The Ama

of the Masters of

the Far East

by

Robert Collier

PO BOX 124

EAST SETAUKET, NY 11733

ROBERT COLLIER PUBLICATIONS, INC.
+1 (408) 540-6573
www.RobertCollierPublications.com

robertcollierpub@aol.com

ISBN 978-0-912576-02-2

CONTENTS

		Page
Chapter I.	POWER WITHIN YOUR GRASP	1
Chapter II.	THE WISDOM OF THE MASTERS	10
Chapter III.	THE POWER OF THOUGHT	33
Chapter IV.	DHARANA—METHOD OF THE MASTERS	58
Chapter V.	THE FIRST SECRET	72
Chapter VI.	THE SECOND SECRET	88
Chapter VII.	THE THIRD SECRET	110
Chapter VIII.	THE FOURTH SECRET	122
Chapter IX.	THE FIFTH SECRET	141
Chapter X.	THE SIXTH SECRET	157
Chapter XI.	THE SEVENTH SECRET	168
Chapter XII.	THE ASANAS—FOR A SOUND BODY	171
Chapter XIII.	BUDDHISM	184
Chapter XIV.	KUNDALINI YOGA	190
Chapter XV.	THE YOGI IDEAL MAN OF CULTURE	209
Chapter XVI.	YOGI TEMPLES	212
	GLOSSARY OF ORIENTAL TERMS AND NAMES	214

CHAPTER I

POWER WITHIN YOUR GRASP

The world is ready to give up its secrets if we only know how to knock, how to give it the necessary blow . . . There is no limit to the power of the human mind.

—SWAMI VIVEKANANDA

For century upon century men have spent their strength and their substance in pursuit of a golden dream. Each age has had a different name for that dream: in olden days it was the philosopher's stone, the Fountain of Youth, Eldorado, the Seven Cities of Cibola: in our own time we call it success, or happiness. Today more millions seek it than ever before, yet in the competitive jungle only a handful seem to be able to find it. Whenever we draw close it melts away, to reappear in the distance, a tantalizing, unattainable will-o'-the-wisp.

Must contentment forever elude us while incessantly it beckons us on? Is this a world where the few are favored and the many are doomed to waste their lives in self-doubt and despair?

Truly our days are passed in worry and trembling. In the summer of our lives we toil mightily, for we know the winter will come. Yet, however hard we labor, our supply does not grow. We are as diligent as ants; and as helpless and obscure in the face of adversity.

We are small; still, inside our hearts each of us has a dream of greatness. It whispers to us that we have tremendous potentialities stored up within, and that, if we knew how to bring them forth, we should be able to rise above our circumstances.

Perhaps it is more than a dream. Sometimes it seems so strong and deep that surely a power mightier than ourselves must have put it there to remind us that we need not be the humble creatures we were born— that security and happiness are our birthright. If only we could find a way to realize our dream of fortune and achievement! If only somehow, somewhere, there were some method, that, faithfully persevered in, would help us to find ourselves and make ourselves the men and women we want to be!

AN ANCIENT METHOD OF MASTERY

Is such a method a fantasy, a mythical philosopher's stone? Yes, says the cynic. But, throughout the East, and in enlightened quarters in the West, loud and numerous are the voices that answer with a resounding no! *No, a wonderful method definitely exists, and has existed for thousands of years!* It was discovered by the Masters of the Far East, the devout holy men dwelling in the remote fastnesses of India and Tibet, in Ceylon and China.

Ages ago the Ancients probed into the heart of Nature and came to understand its innermost mysteries. Not only did the Masters peer through the very fabric of the Universe, animate and inanimate, but they also uncovered the secret principles that rule men's lives. The lore of these Masters enabled them to perform almost incredible feats and attain Heaven on earth. Even today their disciples can gain all the good things a mortal could hope for, drive sickness from their bodies and prolong their youth for great spans of years, win freedom from fear and worry, and lead supremely blissful lives.

MYSTIC CIRCLES OF THE ORIENT

Until the present time, those who wished to learn the method of the Masters had to travel to Asia and find a *guru,* or teacher from whose lips they might receive the sacred wisdom of the ancients. Most of these seekers of the truth have met with disappointment, for the *gurus* are not many in number and each may instruct only a few pupils; the hard-won secrets of the seers may not be passed on to anyone like common merchandise. The man or woman who is accepted for initiation into the mystic circles of the Orient must first acquire a sound knowledge of Sanskrit, the ancient Asiatic language in which the lore of the yogis is taught; the pupil must be pure in heart, and must be willing to undergo a long period of preparation for receiving the secrets of Universal Power.

With the help of this book, however, you can learn the secrets of the Masters without years of study in a foreign land. In only a short while you can hold in your hands the key to powers so amazing that in ages past they were regarded as nothing short of magical. For this book offers you the practices of yoga simplified and brought into conformity with Western ways of thinking, with applications to practical, everyday matters. It follows the principle of the Svetasvatara Upanishad: "Devotion is to be paid to numerous schools and teachers, and the nectar is to be drawn from each of them, as the bee takes nectar from many flowers." It is based upon the teachings of Raja, Karma, and Hatha Yoga as they appear in the Sacred Books of the East, and embodies the profoundest lessons of Gautama Buddha, Patanjali, Swami Vivekananda, Ramakrishna, Mahatma Gandhi, and other Great Masters of the Orient who have lighted torches of wisdom to guide man's faltering footsteps to knowledge and happiness.

RESULTS COME QUICKLY

By applying the wisdom of the Far East, as expounded in this book, you have within your grasp the means to make all of your dreams come true. You can learn to invoke the Law of Supply so that your pockets will never be empty. You can learn to tap immeasurable resources of genius that lie hidden in your subconscious mind—resources that will enable you to forge ahead in your job and increase your earnings tenfold, or found a new business that will bring you success beyond your fondest hopes. You can gain wealth and health and social success; all you want and more.

And don't think there is anything magical involved in acquiring these powers for yourself. It is simply a matter of learning the hidden principles that the Masters have discovered through thousands of years of research and meditation, and applying them for yourself. Results will come quickly as you grow in your powers. You will have immediate, incontrovertible evidence that you can make yourself the happy, effective person you want to be.

The powers of the Master Yogins can easily be yours, if you proceed along the safe and tested ways explained in this book. Here you will find no abracadabra or hocus-pocus, for it is the author's intention to help the reader; not to mystify him. You will not be taught how to charm snakes or do the Indian rope trick, for these are for the most part frauds; practiced by simple tricksters in the hope of earning a few *annas*. But you will learn the laws of psychic energy and mental control that have made the seers of the Far East masters of men since time immemorial.

YOGIC POWERS BRING FAME AND HEALTH

I know of many renowned persons who have learned some of the lore of the Masters and are practicing it right in our own country, and winning fabulous success. One is Yehudi Menuhin, a great concert violinist whose name is world-famous; his concerts are sold out weeks in advance when he appears at Carnegie Hall in New York City. Several of America's favorite screen stars would not think of going on a Hollywood set without practicing meditation as it will be explained in later chapters; for this preparation permits them to enter into their roles as though they were actually the persons whose parts they are playing. The famed screen actress Gloria Swanson, a woman who has reached the middle years, still has the charm, beauty, and suppleness of body of a young girl; thanks to her participation in yogic practices.

Living in the United States today are several

famous British novelists—Aldous Huxley, Christopher Isherwood, and Gerald Heard—men whose books have sold millions of copies and whose scenarios bring fabulous prices from the motion picture studios. Some of the novels they have written have been translated into a dozen foreign languages, and are recognized as world classics in the authors' own lifetimes. These men are profound students of Vedanta, one of the great branches of the wisdom of the Masters of the Far East; the inner enlightenment they derive from their studies has enabled them to release their powers fully and completely, and gain not merely self-fulfillment, but universal acclaim.

RESCUED FROM FAILURE

I could cite many instances of businessmen who have been helped to success through a knowledge of the wisdom of the Orient, but I shall content myself to mention just one who is known to me personally. This man is a publisher with offices located in New York City. The incredibly successful concern he heads grosses millions of dollars annually, and his biography appears in the current issue of *Who's Who;* yet only ten years ago this man's business did not exist and he was an obscure individual in the employ of another.

When this publisher went into business, he was dismayed by the obstacles that blocked his path. His capital was small and his competitors were big. He was worried about losing the little he possessed, and when a decision had to be made, either momentous or trivial, he did not know which way to turn. He was so disturbed that he frequently suffered from digestive upsets and could not sleep at night.

One year he made a business trip to California, and it changed his life. There he was introduced to a swami—not a smooth-tongued fraud but one of the genuine Masters of Oriental Wisdom in the tradition of Sri Aurobindo, Vivekananda, and Ramakrishna, who are revered by millions in India today. This swami did not advertise his wisdom or exact a high price for it; he offered simply to teach a few disciplines of the East because, like all true yogis, he was pledged to the service of his fellow man.

The publisher placed himself in the swami's hands for a few weeks. He learned a number of simple meditative postures and exercises such as will be explained later in this book; the principles of *dharana,* or the Indian technique of concentration, were taught him, and he was given an insight into certain methods of controlling his emotions and releasing latent thought power. When he returned to New York City, he continued to practice these disciplines and soon mastered them. All his worries fell away from him. What had seemed hard had now become easy. His nights and days were suddenly untroubled, and he was able to attack his work with new gusto. He never lacked for ideas or the wisdom to make decisions.

Recently I had lunch with this publisher. In the past he had always complained of the state of his health or of business conditions. But now, on the contrary, he exuded confidence and good cheer. He told me that the banks were only too eager to invest money in his enterprise; successful authors were coming to him from all over the country and begging him to take their books, for they knew he could make more money for them than their present publishers.

A man in his early sixties, he had the vigor and the clear visage of a youth in his twenties. He declared that he could never repay his debt to the swami, but that each year he sent a tithe of his earnings to the holy man in India, where he had his *ashram,* or spiritual retreat; the holy man distributed this money to the poor.

A Science Anyone Can Master

Some people are fortunate enough to discover a few of the secrets of the Masters by themselves, through intuition. The results are often stupendous. Every now and then you will hear of somebody who goes into Wall Street with a few hundred dollars and in a matter of months is a wealthy man. Or there is the case of the young man who is still at college, yet is able to make a scientific discovery or an invention that his professors never even conceived was possible, and reaps a harvest of gold while contributing benefits for all mankind. A middle-aged lady who never put pen to paper earnestly before, suddenly writes a play that stays on Broadway for years, achieving a success that wrings feelings of envy from authors who have written thirty plays, all of which never earned as much in royalties as her single drama.

You can equal or surpass the accomplishments of these happy people without relying upon a chance discovery or an accidental stroke of luck. Long ago the Masters of the Far East reduced luck to a science— a science that anyone can master if he applies himself to it diligently and persistently, and in the right spirit. "Infinite energy," said the Swami Vivekananda, "is at the disposal of everyone, if he only knows how to

8

get it. The yogi has discovered the science of getting it."

No—you need not dread the future, or run before misfortune like an ant scurrying for cover. Peace of mind, financial security, and contentment can be yours almost for the asking, once you know the rules of the Masters and observe them faithfully.

Follow the guidance of the Masters of the Orient, and you can be the architect of your own circumstances. Cement and bricks are nothing but bricks and cement until the architect makes them something more than that. Yesterday, knowing little, with the building materials that were given to you, you could make only a hovel. Tomorrow, knowing much, you will be able to build a stately palace that towers to the skies!

CHAPTER II

THE WISDOM OF THE MASTERS

We are born out of and always remain part of a universe which is a living universe and animated with Spirit . . . at the core is Spirit. That dynamic urge which permeates the universe from centre to circumference we have in ourselves and by it we are continually being acted upon. It burns within us.

SIR FRANCIS YOUNGHUSBAND, K.C.S.I., K.C.I.E.

India has ever been a land of magic and mystery to the West. In older days its fabled treasures of precious metals, ivory, and spices lured Columbus, Vasco da Gama, and other bold mariners across forbidding spans of uncharted ocean. Those who reached their destination found a strange and wondrous land, enormously wealthy not only in material things but in priceless treasures of the spirit.

Many conquerors have stamped across the soil of the subcontinent of India. Two thousand years ago, it was Alexander the Great, who, in 327 B.C., thrust into western India and set up Greek fortresses there. Later Tamerlane and the Moguls came; then the French, the Dutch, and the British, who warred with one another for the rich spoils of India. For a long time the conquerors held sway. But, as all history relates, not one of them lasted. In the end the ancient faith corroded the chains of the enslavers; their armed might and materialistic beliefs dissolved like a mist in the morning sun.

The strength of the Orient is the strength of the spirit. We Westerners place our reliance in cannon and aircraft and atomic bombs; the Oriental leans confidently upon the resources of his soul. His victories are greater than ours, even though his means appear invisible. The people of India, by a massive effort of the spirit, were able to compel the British to leave their shores. Their leader was no general, but a holy man, a mahatma, and the doctrine he preached was one of the purest spirituality. Mahatma Gandhi was able to free 400,000,000 Indians from almost two centuries of British rule.

The psychic force of the Hindus is difficult for us to understand, for we Westerners, though we pay lip-service to spirituality, believe primarily in things that we can see and feel. Ours is the cult of the concrete; we worship machines and money and science. In our society the high priests are the technical specialists, the experts who are the masters of our machines, our finances, and our science.

EXPERTS IN THE SPIRITUAL

The Hindus are specialists, too. They are experts in the spiritual as we are in the material. For four thousand years they have been studying the spirit and the unseen forces that make and mold the universe.

They have discovered hidden laws and powers whose existence our most advanced scientists have only begun to suspect. They have achieved a degree of control over their bodies and spirits that has been possible only to a handful of men in the West.

Reports of the incredible powers of the yogis, or sages of India, appear often in the daily press of the United States and Europe. We have all heard of holy men who are able to lie upon beds of nails for days and then arise with their flesh uncut. We read of Indian holy men who allow themselves to be completely buried, without air, food, or drink for days; when they are exhumed, they soon come back to life, apparently unharmed by their superhuman experience.

YOGIS ARE LONG-LIVED

If you go to India, you may see for yourself the accomplishments of its seers. On some of the holy days, fairs are held in many sections of India. At these celebrations, anyone is welcome to converse with the sages who are present, surrounded by hordes of adulants who have come from near and far to pay their respects to these saintly figures.

These seers, whose lives are devoted to the cultivation of the spirit, are often women as well as men. Some of them, you will learn, are, despite their youthful appearance and well-developed bodies, persons of great age. It is not unusual to see a sage who hardly looks more than forty years of age, yet is reported to be well past the century mark. These gifted people look forward with confidence to many more years of life. They believe that with purity of spirit they gain great power over their physical bodies.

In India, you will hear reports of persons who have lived as much as two hundred years or possibly longer, vying with the patriarchs of the Old Testament in longevity. These persons have withdrawn from ordinary life, and spend their days in meditation. Many are said to dwell in caves in the Himalayas. They are considered the most knowledgeable of *gurus,* or teachers, and it is related that they possess the power to foretell and to control the future, and also to transfer their thoughts.

Yoga Is Soul Control

Some readers will naturally greet such stories with skepticism, nor can I blame them. We are prone to disbelieve things that are in contradiction to the evidence of our own senses. Still, one should not rule out the possibility of truth here. People pooh-poohed Edison's statement that he would one day be able to light up a whole city simply by throwing a switch. Today the truth of his assertion is so manifest that nobody bothers to think twice about the wonder of electricity. Our recently discovered ability to send words and pictures in full color through the air would probably have struck our forebears as witchcraft of a high order. The yogis, by the way, do not lay claim to supernatural powers; on the contrary, they merely state that they have mastered the scientific control of the psyche or soul—in their own language, *kaivalya.*

Yoga Sutras of Patanjali

One of the most significant books of the Orient is called the Yoga Sutras or Yoga Aphorisms of Patanjali. Patanjali, a deeply revered teacher of the Far

East, lived before the birth of Christ. Although his very identity is obscured by the mists of time, his brief book shows perennial vigor. It has been studied by millions in India, and has shown them the way to greater power. We shall have occasion to refer to it again and again in the course of this work, for it is both profound and to the point.

BRAHMA, SOUL OF THE UNIVERSE

The word yoga means "yoke"—the yoking of the individual to the great forces of Nature and the Universe. Patanjali, Shankara, and other Masters of the Far East teach that all the Universe is one. In the words of the Upanishads, the sacred Vedic books of ancient India, "There is one Ruler, the Spirit that is in all things, who transforms his one form into many." This Ruler we of the West call God, the Hindus Brahma. In the Hindu view, He is not only the Master of the Universe—He is the Universe itself, and all things in it. The Judaeo-Christian Scriptures, which describe God as the Creator of all things, are in fundamental agreement with this concept.

The Masters of the East teach that the Universe is an infinite reservoir of power and energy. Its force and persistence blaze forth in the eternally burning sun and stars, in the millions of giant galaxies and nebulae that illuminate the endless stretches of space. Not only does this vast Power show itself to us in heavenly bodies of enormous magnitude; if we look at the smallest thing that is, the atom, we observe in the ceaseless motion of its protons and electrons the same boundless, inexhaustible energy, the soul of Brahma. We discover it wherever we turn: in the

14

blade of grass and in the flower that grows from a tiny, life-laden seed, flourishes for a season, then dies, and is born again. We see this regenerative force in the life of man, who, though he is born to die, can create other creatures in his image. It is with Brahma, the Soul of the Universe, that the yogis seek union.

The Power of Supply Is in Man

The Universe is Brahma, but man, being part of the Universe is Brahma, too, once he can realize the potentially divine within him.

The yogis say—to quote one of the greatest of them, the Swami Vivekananda—that "desires and wants are in man, that the power of supply is also in man." The Yoga Sutras and the other Sacred Books of the East lay down a system for achieving union with the Infinite and drawing upon this infinite treasure-house of supply. They teach that the subtle or refined has great power over the gross, or, as we would say it, that mind has power over matter. This we observe every moment of our lives. It is the mind that regulates and commands the body. It is our organized thought processes, converted into dynamos, steamshovels, locomotives, airplanes, tractors and other mechanical contrivances, that have subdued Nature and made her obedient to our beck and call.

But the Masters of the Far East go even further. They declare that by refining our minds, we can become capable of direct contact with *prana,* or Infinite Energy, which science tells us is the true essence of matter. Drawing upon the Energy of the Universe, not only does our mind become capable of infinitely greater performance—unleashing energies we never dreamed we possessed—but we can bend matter to our will.

Powers Easily Achieved

We have already seen that yoga, as practiced by the Masters, is no easy discipline. It has many branches, and one has to devote a lifetime to its study if he would perfect himself in it. (For that matter, perfection cannot be absolutely attained, although the greatest of the Masters have come close to it.)

The arduousness of yoga need not discourage us, however. We shall content ourselves in this book to gain only some of the minor powers. They are easily achieved and are enough to bring the fulfillment of most earthly wishes. True, what we shall attempt would be little to one of the Master Yogins of the Far East—but it will be much for us if it brings us happiness and the realization of long-cherished dreams.

For the Masters, the ability to wrest of life the physical things they want of it is only the first step. As they proceed in their studies, over the years, they go much further than we who live amid the hustle and bustle of a materialistic culture can ever hope to. They learn, through purification of the body and control of the mind, to transcend human consciousness and to achieve union with Brahma. They acquire powers that they term *siddhis,* and that we in the West have traditionally considered occult. Most Americans have heard of these powers and are curious about them, so we shall glance at them before launching directly into our study of the method of the Masters.

A CHANNEL OF UNIVERSAL POWER

As a fine magnifying glass concentrates the rays of the sun and produces a fire, so the refined mind of the yogi concentrates the Infinite Energy of the Universe and causes it to do his bidding. Through meditation and soul control, he becomes a channel of Universal Power, which he is able to regulate and make flow where he will. In the language of India, this ability is known as *samyama*. The true Masters learn, by degrees, to make *samyama* upon all of Nature or any part of it.

The Yoga Sutras of Patanjali tell us that by making *samyama* upon the hollow of his throat, a yoga can cause hunger to disappear. When a yogi makes *samyama* upon *udana,* the Hindu name for a vital nerve-current in the lungs, he can make his body lighter and perform many remarkable feats. This, the Masters tell us, was the power exercised by Jesus when He walked upon the waters. It is the way they explain the well-known ability of the holy men of the Far East to rest upon a bed of nails for long periods of time or walk along a pathway strewn with hot coals. Many of the Masters have been able to foretell the hour of their death; according to Patanjali's Sutras, through control of the nerve-current *udana* a yogi can die at will.

FORCE OF THE SPIRIT

A great variety of other *samyamas* lie at the disposal of the adept, according to Patanjali. A certain form of the body is known as *akasa;* this is its immaterial form, or, as we would put it, the astral body. By

17

making *samyama* upon the *akasa,* the yogi is able to separate this spiritual body from the body of flesh, bone, and blood; he now has the power to travel where he will, in the spirit.

In recent years a number of Europeans have come to India and scaled Everest, Annapurna, Godwin Austen, and other great mountains that tower over 25,000 feet to the sky in the north of that ancient land. Possibly you have read of the intrepid men who toiled up the craggy sides of those stony giants. Marvel as we will at the heroism and fortitude of the mountain climbers—their achievements are regarded as epochal in the West—the holy men of northern India and Tibet find them not only unimpressive, but hardly worthy of comment. They declare that they have been to the summits of these mountains on countless occasions, and offer detailed descriptions of the peaks and their surrounding area as evidence. They say that the efforts expended by the Westerners were praiseworthy, yet completely unnecessary—an astral body is considerably lighter than a physical one, and travels so much faster!

THE QUALITY OF QUIETNESS

The Masters of the Far East also possess the ability to make themselves invisible. When the Tashi Lama, one of the great religious leaders of Tibet, passed some time in India, he gave a remarkable demonstration of his supernormal abilities.

Oddly enough, he had been asked by some visitors whether he possessed any supernatural powers, and his only reply had been a smile. Not long afterward, the gentlemen of his household and his personal bodyguard, who had been standing all about him, suddenly became aware that he had disappeared. Terror gripped their hearts, for they were entrusted with his safety; if any harm came to him, they would have to answer with their lives.

Now began a mad search. Every inch of the garden, the house, and the surrounding grounds was ransacked, yet no trace of the missing lama could be found. Many minutes passed as the soldiers milled about, looking for their lost leader, when suddenly one of the officers perceived that the Tashi Lama was sitting in the midst of the wild melee, a smile of playful amusement on his benign features.

Had the lama actually vanished? Not really; but he had, by the exercise of yogic powers, obliterated his form so that his followers could not see him. Patanjali has said that "by making *samyama* on the shape or outline of the body, its form becomes impossible to perceive, and the eye is deprived of its capacity for seeing." We of the West might ascribe it to the superb quietness that the yogi is capable of; he can all at once sink into such immobility that his presence is lost, blending indistinguishably with his surroundings. In this state of quietness, he refreshes his mind and body.

THOUGHT TRANSFERENCE AND YOGA

By making *samyama* on the "light of the heart," says Patanjali—that is, by the use of psychic powers which have been the property of gifted or saintly persons in all ages—the yogi gains a knowledge of the remote or faraway. He is able to observe events that are occurring in other cities or even in countries on the other side of the world.

Yogis can also telegraph mental messages to people in distant places. This, of course, is the power we know as telepathy. In the West telepathy is now receiving serious scientific study and the experiments of Professor J. B. Rhine of Duke University have satisfied many that telepathy is a distinct possibility; in the Orient it is taken for granted, and proofs of its reality have been offered for thousands of years.

Telepathy or thought transference is also an instance of *samyama*—in this case, *samyama* upon the mind of another. Most well-read persons are familiar with the writings of Maxim Gorky, one of Russia's outstanding novelists of the early twentieth century; his books *The Lower Depths* and *Mother* have been made into masterful motion pictures. Gorky was fond of relating an experience he once had with a Hindu, in Caucasia. The Indian showed the novelist an album with metallic pages that were quite blank. As Gorky examined the pages, shapes and colors began to appear on them. As he looked, they took definite forms, and he realized he was beholding the great cities of India, just as though their pictures were actually printed on the pages.

Gorky, you may recall, was a died-in-the wool materialist, and he examined the book to see if it had been treated with chemicals that would make the pictures appear when the book was opened. He was convinced that he had encountered an authentic case of thought transference.

Miracle of Telekinesis

The Yoga Sutras state that telekinesis also becomes possible as one's mastery grows. Telekinesis (derived from two Greek words signifying "far motion") is the moving or control of objects at a distance, without recourse to physical means. The Army is now able, by radio, to guide unmanned robot aircraft and aerial torpedoes to a selected goal. The yogi, according to Patanjali, can achieve the same result by concentration.

That the brain does produce electrical energy is a well-known fact. Every day, in their examining rooms, brain specialists measure the electrical charges within the craniums of their patients to determine whether any pathological condition is present. Can we say it is inconceivable that certain gifted persons, through secret techniques, should be able to amplify the discharge of electricity in their brains and bring it to bear upon objects outside their bodies? The great electrical wizard Charles Steinmetz has said: "The most important advance in the next fifty years will be in the realm of the spiritual—dealing with the spirit—thought."

The Saddhu and the Train

The Hindus offer many evidences of the reality of telekinesis. Take, for example, the case of the saddhu, or holy man, who stopped a train.

In India it is common to see saddhus, who, following the example of Buddha and other Eastern saints, have renounced all worldly possessions, and gain their livelihood by teaching and begging alms; they are profoundly revered by the populace. Railroads, however, take a different view of such penniless folk, and, one day, when a saddhu climbed aboard a train, it was promptly discovered that he had no ticket, and he was put off.

The engineer then began to start the locomotive. He whipped up the steam, but the train refused to roll. A quick inspection revealed there was nothing mechanically wrong. The engineer took his seat again and did all that was necessary to put the train in motion. Still the great wheels refused to turn.

Now the passengers, who were persons of simple faith and great understanding, began to call: "The saddhu! The saddhu! The train will not move until he is back aboard." The conductor got down and fetched the holy man, who had been standing quietly beside the track. No sooner was he aboard than the train gave a lurch and began to move forward.

Is telekinesis unbelievable? Perhaps so. But so were television, teletypewriters, and the telephone before they were invented. Perhaps tomorrow the General Electric research laboratories will issue a report declaring that their engineers have developed a method for making psychic energy effective at a distance. Then "black magic" will become "white."

The Cloud of Virtue

These powers, and many others described in the Yoga Sutras, remarkable though they are, are not the ultimate goal of the yogi. They are high, but they are not the highest achievement of which he is capable. As a matter of fact, they are a hindrance to the yogi; after he has mastered the *samyamas* and other *siddhis*, he must compel himself to renounce them as well as all earthly wishes, and take the next step. The Sacred Books of the East refer to this as *kaivalya,* liberation, or "the cloud of virtue." It is defined as true spiritual consciousness—a state of infinite freedom. In this condition the Master has all knowledge within his grasp, and has reached a state of self-realization and sublimity that can only be compared to that of the angels.

The Masters of the Far East cultivate their powers only for good purposes. Their hearts are set upon the welfare and progress not only of man, but of all living things. All the teachings of the East—the words of the Bhagavad Gita, the Rigvedas, of Buddha, Confucius, and other great teachers—lay great emphasis upon the cultivation of kindliness, upon striving for perfection in the highest terms conceived of in Western religion. The Hindu seers discovered the moving force of the Universe thousands of years ago, and they say that it tends toward good, and that only the good are in tune with it. The man whose thoughts and aspirations are wicked will never attain to the higher powers.

The Masters and Christianity

"I am realizing every day," wrote Mahatma Gandhi, "that the search for truth is vain unless it is founded on love . . . To injure a single human being is to injure those divine powers within us, and thus the harm reaches not only that one human being, but with him the whole world." This passage, like many other utterances and aphorisms of the seers of the Orient, is remarkably reminiscent of the sayings of Jesus.

Indeed, there is nothing in the wisdom of the Orient,

in its purest form, as taught by the Masters of the East, that is repugnant to Christianity. The Masters have always shown the greatest sympathy for Christianity; many Hindus even go so far as to claim Jesus for their own, pointing out that he was born in Palestine, which is a part of Asia, and not in Europe. They remind us that the Three Magi, or Wise Kings of the East, were Asiatics, and were singled out by God to have foreknowledge of the birth of Jesus, and followed the Star across distant deserts until they found Him in Bethlehem.

The Masters of the Far East discovered, untold ages ago, that there is but one God. The simple people of India may pay reverence to many deities—Brahma, Vishnu, Siva, and others—but all represent various aspects of the Great Force That Moves the Universe. The Masters say that God is known to the different peoples of the earth in many different shapes and under many different names, but that He is always the same God and is absolutely One. They point out that the saints and sages of all lands and times draw their strength and power from Him, no matter by what name He is known—Brahma to the Hindus, Ahura Mazda to the Persians, Manito to the American Indians, Allah to the Mohammedans, Jehovah to the Jews. Mahatma Gandhi said: "I can detect no inconsistency in declaring that I can, without in any way whatsoever impairing the dignity of Hinduism, pay equal homage to the best of Islam, Christianity, Zoroastrianism, and Judaism."

"Even as a tree has a single trunk, but many branches and leaves," declared the Mahatma on another occasion, "so is there one true and perfect religion, but it becomes many, as it passes through the human medium. The one religion is beyond all speech. Imperfect men put it into such language as they can command and their words are interpreted by other men equally imperfect. Whose interpretation is to be held to be the right one? . . . . True knowledge of religion breaks down the barriers between faith and faith."

RAMAKRISHNA'S VISION OF JESUS

The Masters of the East, as already suggested, feel a special affinity to Jesus. Many of them place him with Buddha in the hierarchy of Master Yogins, worshipping him with a fervor that has been equalled only by the saints. To some He has come in visions, as He did to Paul in the desert. Sir Francis Younghusband, who spent many years in the Orient, gives us a deeply moving account of how Ramakrishna, one of India's holiest men, after long purification of his soul, came face to face with Jesus:

"On the fourth day he was walking in the grove when he suddenly saw an extraordinary-looking person of serene aspect approaching with his gaze intently fixed on him. He knew at once that he was not a Hindu. He had large, beautiful eyes, and, though the nose was different from an Indian's, it in no way marred the comeliness of his face. Ramakrishna was charmed, and wondered who it might be. Presently the figure drew near. Then, from the inmost recesses of Ramakrishna's heart there went up the note, 'This is Christ who poured out His heart's blood for the redemption of mankind and suffered agonies for its sake. It is none else than that Master Yogin, Jesus, the embodiment of Love.'

"Then the Son of Man embraced Ramakrishna and became merged in him. Ramakrishna lost outward consciousness . . .

"After some time he came back to normal consciousness and was convinced that Jesus Christ was an Incarnation of the Lord."

JESUS IN THE ORIENT

The life of Gautama Buddha, the Enlightened One of the East, reveals incredible parallels with the life of Jesus. Like Jesus, Buddha devoted his life to wandering across the face of the land, teaching immortal truths to the people and healing the sick. The Abbé Huc, who over a century ago provided us with our first reliable account of life in Tartary and Tibet, says that on his journey through the holy land of the lamas he found that they readily accepted the sayings of Jesus for they already knew things very much like them from the Buddhist Scriptures. In the Potala, the palace of the Dalai Lama, the Abbé conferred with the Regent of Tibet. "Thy faith," the Regent told him, "is like unto ours. Our difference is only in the explanations."

Some of the lamas, who hand down ancient traditions, say that it is a historical fact that Jesus actually visited India and Tibet. In the language of the Orient His name is transcribed as Issa. The lamas say that Issa, as a youth, left Joseph and Mary for a while and journeyed with some merchants of Jerusalem in the direction of the Indus. They relate that He sowed

His words at Benares, in Nepal, and in the Himalayas. In Tibet the Buddhist monks welcomed Him as a teacher of the divine truths, and the wretched and miserable flocked about Him wherever He appeared; His minstrations brought miraculous recovery to the lame, the halt, and the blind.

Concerning the oriental travels of Jesus the New Testament is silent. Still, it is undeniable that the four Gospels offer us only a fragmentary account of the Greatest Life Ever Lived; little that tells of His early years has come down to us, if indeed it was ever recorded by the humble folk that knew Him.

Of the few white persons who have visited Tibet, several have noted that the fish is often seen as a decoration on religious objects and buildings; this same symbol, carved out by the early Christian martyrs, may be viewed in the catacombs where they hid in Rome, during the years of persecution. The fish was used by the early Christians as a symbol of their faith because the word in Greek—*ichthys*—has in it the first letters of the Greek words for "Jesus Christ, Son of God."

There are many other echoes of Jesus and His followers in the lands of the East. Westerners who have been permitted to enter the great lamaseries of Tibet, where the ancient wisdom of the Masters is taught, have been struck by the similarity of these oriental monasteries to those of the West. In them one observes the same piety, the same worship of goodness and devotion to God. The holy men fast and live in retirement from the world; their benedictions, their sacred songs, their religious services are not unlike those observed in a European or American cathedral.

Tsong-Kapa's Mysterious Teacher

In the east of Tibet stands the huge Kumbum lamasery, the dwelling place of thousands of yellow-cap lamas. One of the most sacred religious centers of all Tibet, Kumbum is especially renowned as the birthplace of Tsong-Kapa, a major seer and lama of five centuries ago. It was Tsong-Kapa who breathed fresh vitality into the old teachings of Buddha, when there was a danger that they might become lost in empty ritual. And the monks of Kumbum tell that Tsong-Kapa drew his wisdom and courage from a stranger who had come from the West. They say this teacher was a man of great piety and learning, with flashing eyes and a large nose, such as one does not see in the highlands of Tibet. Some of the monks believe it may have been an incarnation of Jesus Himself, or one of His followers, that showed Tsong-Kapa the way.

The Kinship of East and West

The faiths of the East and West are closely allied, just as their political destinies are destined to be in the years ahead. The Sacred Books of the East and the profound and inspiring thoughts they express are not alien to us, for we knew them of old.

Thousands of years ago, the peoples of the East and West were one, dwelling in the same habitations and speaking the same tongue. The great folk stocks of Europe and America and the Aryans of India once dwelt together in eastern Europe. From their prehistoric home some groups of these Indo-European peoples moved westward in great migratory waves, while others journeyed to the East. For almost a thousand years, starting in 2,000 B.C., tides of them swept into the Greek mainland, where they built marvelous temples and palaces. Numbers went into the valley of the Danube and then spread to the north and the west, bringing with them herds of cattle and flocks of sheep, and their belief in a God in the sky. These people became the ancestors of the Celts, the Scandinavians, the Germans, and other European groups. Others invaded Italy, where their descendants built the Roman Empire. Yet another wave of Indo-Europeans poured down upon the subcontinent of India. These we know as the Aryans. They came about 2,500 B.C.

Understanding the Hindus

The native people of India were a dark-skinned race, the Dravidians. Although they had achieved a good degree of civilization, they could not withstand the onslaught of the invading Indo-Europeans. In time the Dravidians were subdued by them and became their serfs.

Ages ago, the famed castes of India began to arise. Highest of all were the priests, or Brahmins, who interpreted the ancient Sacred Books, the Vedas. Next were the warriors, or Kshatriya caste, the nobles who ruled the land. After these came the Vaisyas—the merchants, propertied farmers, herdsmen, artisans, and lenders of money. Last of the four castes was the Sudra, who were serfs and servants. Outside the castes were the persons of no caste—the pariahs. Castes came to be hereditary. It is interesting to note that the Hindu word for caste is *varna,* or "color"; the ancient system doubtless was based upon the color differences

29

between Aryans and Dravidians, but the color line became obscured as they intermarried.

Over the centuries the castes divided and subdivided again and again. Today there are no fewer than seven thousand. The pariahs, of whom there are more than 50,000,000 in India today, have up till the present led wretched lives, without hope of improvement. But things are looking up for them now. The government of modern India, much like our own government, is working to eradicate caste and color lines, and alleviate the lot of the untouchables. It has taken to heart the thought of Gandhi, the Master Yogin, who said: "It has always been a mystery to me how men can feel themselves honored by the humiliation of their fellow beings."

BROTHERS IN LANGUAGE AND THOUGHT

The people of India and the people of Europe and America are very different in appearance and culture —they have been separated for thousands of years— but a fundamental kinship of thought and language still survives. The ancient Hindus spoke Sanskrit, the tongue of the Vedas and the Masters of the Far East. But their word *matr* is still recognizably our word *mother.* The Hindu word for a potentate is *rajah;* the Romans used the same word, changed a bit—*rex;* it still survives for us in the related word in our language, *rich,* and the German word *Reich.* Their ancient writings of holy wisdom, the Vedas, bear in their name the same root as our word *wits.* The word *sutras,* which now means "aphorisms," originally meant a "thread" and then a "string of rules"; scholars tell

30

us it is closely related to our word "sew." Many other words have the same fraternal relationship. But stronger than the kinship of language is that of thought and religion. The ancient Aryans, like Americans and Europeans today, believed in a Heavenly Father, whom they called in their language *Dyaush pitar* (the name is closely related to that of Jupiter, supreme deity of the Romans). As the distinguished Orientalist, Professor F. Max Müller, has written:

"Thousands of years have passed since the Aryan nations separated to travel to the north and the south, the west and the east; they have each formed languages, they have each founded empires and philosophies, they have each built temples and razed them to the ground; they have all grown older, and it may be wiser and better; but when they search for a name for what is most exalted and yet most dear to every one of us, when they wish to express both awe and love, the infinite and the finite, they can but do what their old fathers did when gazing up to the eternal sky, and feeling the presence of a Being as far as far, and as near as near can be, they can but combine the selfsame words, and utter once more the primeval Aryan prayer, Heaven-Father, in that form which will endure forever: 'Our Father which art in heaven.' "

We are bound to the East by innumerable ties; in pages of history yet to be written, we shall be bound still more closely. One of the transcendental values the Orient can give us is her wisdom, which she has kept pure and undefiled. The teachings of her wise men can show us not only the way to health and prosperity, but to spiritual contentment as well. For the

Masters of the Far East teach us that each soul is divine, and they show us a method for manifesting the divine that dwells inside each of us, by controlling Nature in ourselves and in the world about us. They show us the way to freedom and greater power.

CHAPTER III

THE POWER OF THOUGHT

> All that we are is the result of what we have thought:
> it is founded on our thoughts, it is made up of our
> thoughts. If a man speaks or acts with an evil thought,
> pain follows him, as the wheel follows the foot of the
> ox that draws the carriage.
> All that we are is the result of what we have thought:
> it is founded on our thoughts, it is made up of our
> thoughts. If a man speaks or acts with a pure thought,
> happiness follows him, like a shadow that never leaves
> him.
>
> —GAUTAMA BUDDHA

Not long ago, a group of scientists and journalists
assembled at the Bell Telephone Laboratories at
Murray Hill, New Jersey, to witness an astonishing
demonstration.

The objects displayed for the inspection of the
curious guests might not have seemed very impressive
at first glance. One part of the exhibit was a toy ferris
wheel which turned and turned without winding. Another feature was two small radio transmitters which
sent voice and music signals. Over a simple telephone
unit, two men engaged in a conversation.

For all these mechanisms, the power was provided

by batteries. These were ordinary-looking affairs. They were made of strips of silicon, an ingredient of common sand. They possessed no moving parts.

But they drew their power from the sun!

The Bell Laboratories say that *nothing is consumed or destroyed in the operation of their batteries, and that they should last indefinitely!*

Can you conceive how historic an event that demonstration is likely to prove?

Since the dawn of the Industrial Revolution, when man first learned the secret of making large-scale mechanical power do the work he had been accustomed to performing with his own hands, he has been exhausting the physical resources of the earth at a tremendous rate. The earth contains only a given amount of coal and oil, and every year these priceless stores of power are consumed in greater quantity by our dynamos and machines. Some experts believe that more than half of our total reserves of coal and oil have already been used up; what remains may not last us more than another fifty years.

Toward the close of World War II the hopes of conservationists were raised by the discovery of a new fuel substitute—the energy locked inside the uranium atom. Unfortunately, however, the uranium used for the production of atomic power is exceedingly scarce; that is why it brings so high a price. The hope that it will replace coal and oil when these are gone is chimerical—the earth's supply of uranium ore may well be exhausted long before the available supplies of coal and oil.

But not the power of the sun! Scientists tell us that great star, which since the beginning of things has been emitting energy in the form of light and heat, will not be exhausted for a long time. They estimate that it will take about 150,000,000,000 years before it has burnt up even one per cent of its mass. *Each day it sends us almost as much energy as is contained in all the reserves of uranium, coal, and oil known to exist!*

When the earth's bowels have been emptied of its precious supply of coal, oil, and uranium, we shall be able to produce electricity to keep our machines moving, our homes warm, and our cars and planes traveling, thanks to the discovery of the science of utilizing solar power. Our children's children will not have to burn their furniture for light, or huddle together to keep from freezing.

A Thought Came to Them

The science of harnessing the energy of the sun is only in its infancy. Its adulthood, however, will mean a new age of freedom and ease for mankind. This discovery is unquestionably one of the most remarkable in history. Yet even more remarkable is the fact that it has come so late.

For the estimated million years of his existence on earth, man has bathed himself in the sun, and drawn health and vigor from it. He has used it to grow wheat for his bread and corn for his pigs. He has reckoned his days and years by it, felt cheerful when it shone and sad when it hid its face behind clouds. It was right over his head—yet he completely overlooked it as a source of energy to be converted into mechanical power!

In the annals of human progress, the men of science

who developed the principles of the use of solar energy may well be described as geniuses. No doubt they possess many outstanding qualities—yet one is of much greater importance than the rest. These men were able to look at the obvious—a thing that billions of their fellows had passed by without a second glance—and see something in it that was not obvious. A thought came to them that did not come to other men: the thought of harnessing the seething strength of the sun. By putting that thought into practical application, they have earned the undying gratitude of the human race.

Ideas Revolutionize the World

It is thoughts that make our world. Historians say that electricity, the automobile, the airplane, and atomic energy have revolutionized life in the twentieth century. So they have—but before each of these there was an idea.

Every man that ever lived (and possessed the power to see) has watched birds in flight. There are very few, however, who, like Leonardo da Vinci and the Wright Brothers, have taken the trouble to think seriously about flight. When these men thought, and thought hard, their idea of a flying machine was born. In the final analysis, it was a thought that made human flight possible.

The electric light was no chance discovery. As a young man, Thomas Alva Edison acquired a background in the principles of electricity. He recognized that this marvelous force, which even today is only vaguely understood, could be put to work in many remarkable ways. He looked at the candles and gas lights that were used in his time and saw how annoying and unreliable they were. The idea was born in his mind that he could, by using electricity, power a lamp that would be far superior to any means of illumination then known.

For close to ten years Edison kept this idea in his mind. He made a glass lamp, and in it he tried one substance after another in an effort to find one that would burn for a long time, but none was satisfactory. He sent his people to every part of the earth to search for the proper material for his lamp. Thousands of different substances were forwarded to his laboratory from foreign lands. Each was painstakingly tested, with no success. Finally, after he had spent over $40,000 and an amount of effort beyond the capabilities of ordinary men, he managed to produce a lamp that would burn for all of forty hours. His idea had at last been translated into partial reality. Further thought and testing created the superb electric lamp of today.

The history of other inventions and discoveries is much the same. Take, as another example, Isaac Newton and the law of gravitation. A man once asked the great English scientist how he happened to discover it. His answer? "By thinking about it all the time."

Lengthened Shadows of Our Thoughts

It is thoughts and ideas, not objects, that have revolutionized the world. Ralph Waldo Emerson, one of America's most noted thinkers, once remarked that "an institution is the lengthened shadow of a man." He had in mind the fact that Mohammedanism directly reflects the work of Mohammed, Christianity the work of Jesus, Protestantism the work of Martin

Luther. But each of these great figures of world religion had thoughts before he began the work for which he became famous. Thoughts made the man, then the institution.

Every action, if it is not instinctual or produced by habit, is preceded by thought. Not only our institutions, but everything we have ever done or will do, for good or bad, is the lengthened shadow of our thoughts.

FATHER OF THE DEED

Thoughts are the fathers of deeds. You cannot achieve success or happiness in the world unless you have thoughts that are conducive to happiness or success.

Look closely at the lives of the people about you, and you will see that, wherever their paths have led them, their thoughts went on before. Pasteur did not become a great chemist without first devoting all his thoughts to chemistry. John D. Rockefeller, Sr., did not become a millionaire without thinking about money and the ways and means of acquiring it. Through their concentrated thoughts these men achieved what they wanted most out of life.

The chief difference between the man who makes the grade in life and the man who does not, lies in their thoughts. The person who was a shipping clerk at age eighteen, and is still tying packages and shifting boxes at age fifty-eight, may complain about his hard luck—but generally he has only himself to blame. The precise reason for his failure lies in his mind; not in his circumstances. He never seriously thought of himself as being anything but a shipping clerk. Of course he would have liked to own the business that employed him, or to gain wealth in some other way. But he never held such thoughts earnestly or kept them steadfast in mind. Had he been seriously dissatisfied, had he converted his discontent into constructive channels, there is little doubt that he would have amounted to something. Shakespeare's memorable lines place the responsibility where it belongs: "The fault, dear Brutus, lies not in our stars, but in ourselves that we are underlings."

This truth was realized thousands of years ago by the Masters of the Far East. In the words of the Upanishads, the ancient books of Hindu wisdom, "A man becomes what he thinks."

THOUGHT AND CHARACTER

A man's character, generally speaking, is not separable from the thoughts he has; a man's thoughts *are* his character. And it is equally true that a direct relationship exists between the circumstances in which a person habitually finds himself and the kind of thinking that goes on inside his head.

Whatever your situation in life, it is a reflection of your inner being and the kind of thoughts you have. The thoughts, either helpful or damaging, that you have allowed to take root in your mind and that you have nurtured there either consciously or unconsciously, have determined your lot with all the accuracy of a mathematical principle.

Metaphysicians are in the habit of calling this principle the Law of Attraction. They point out that the mind attracts to itself those things or circumstances that appeal to it; it is as though they already

39

existed in it in embryo. Thus, the fears in your mind will sooner or later be turned into reality, if they are strong enough; so, too, will be the things your mind cherishes. "Circumstances," says the metaphysician, "are the means by which the soul receives its own."

THOUGHT OVER ENVIRONMENT

We do not have to look far to discover examples of people who have refused to be satisfied with the circumstances in which they were born. Our history is full of the epic achievements of such men. Two of the most forceful figures that ever occupied the White House, Andrew Jackson and Abraham Lincoln, came of exceedingly humble origins. Although born poor, they realized they could make their own circumstances. In lifting themselves up, they were of service not only to themselves, but to their country.

Of course, simply wanting to get ahead is no guarantee that a man will reach his goal. The wish comes first, but it must be strong enough to generate the energy and persistence that serve to make a man irresistible. "Fortune," says an old Sanskrit proverb, "attendeth that lion amongst men who exerteth himself; they are weak men who declare Fate to be the sole cause."

The career of Thomas Jonathan Jackson—"Stonewall" Jackson, one of the most famous and inspired generals of all time—offers a superb example of the power of thought over environment. Every step of the way, Jackson consciously nurtured thoughts that would help him to better his lot.

Tom Jackson's childhood hardly betokened great achievements. He was orphaned early in life, and his parents' death left him completely unprovided for. What little education he had was received at a small school in the rural South.

This poor boy burned with the desire to make something of himself. He wanted to become an officer in the United States Army. Nomination to enter West Point, then as now, lay in the hands of the local Congressman. And what Congressman would think of nominating humble Tom Jackson, when the son of a fine old Southern family with considerable political influence wanted to get into the Military Academy? Tom's chances of becoming an Army officer did not look very promising.

Still, if your thought is strong enough, it will find a way to project itself into reality. Your thought will make you so sensitive to opportunity, that you will hear opportunity before it knocks.

Another boy had been preferred to Tom for the West Point nomination. That boy rode off gaily to the famed soldier school on the Hudson. When he got there, however, he found that the military life was more than handsome uniforms, colorful parades, and dates with admiring beauties. Discipline was severe; the studies were arduous; the life was all hard work, day and night, with a minimum of glamour. The boy soon had more than he could take. He tendered his resignation and headed for home.

When Tom heard the news, he sprang into action. He had no powerful friends, but by dint of his sincerity and earnestness he was able to win support from total strangers; he was named as a replacement for the youth who had dropped out.

Like a fire-breathing dragon, a strenuous entrance examination still blocked the gates of the Academy to Tom. But this boy who wanted to get ahead did not know the meaning of discouragement. He had always used idle moments to fill his head with information that his meager education had denied him. To this store of knowledge he added now, by intensive study. He took the examination and passed.

Tom Jackson, when he first appeared at the academy, standing among the smartly turned-out recruits from well-to-do homes, was hardly a prepossessing figure. He seemed ill at ease and gawky in his poor country clothes. But he had something more important to advancement in the military than fine clothing: he had determined with his heart and soul that he would succeed and he was prepared to back up his resolution with indefatigable effort.

Those who had been amused at the poor figure Jackson cut in his first days at West Point soon had occasion to stifle their laughter. He shone in his classes and on the parade ground. He did better than his fellow students because he worked harder, driven by a sense of his deficiencies.

Each evening, as the hour for taps approached, young Jackson used to carry coals to the stove in his dormitory. He piled them so high that the fire was almost extinguished. When the signal was given to put out the lights, however, there was a bright blaze going in his stove. Young Jackson moved his books to the floor next to the stove and there, in the ruddy glow, put in extra hours of study while his classmates slept. Only when the coal was consumed, and the gloom became too deep for him to see any longer, did he crawl into bed.

"You May Be Whatever You Resolve to Be"

One of Tom Jackson's favorite sayings in those days sums up the story of his life. Like George Washington and Benjamin Franklin before him, he wrote a list of rules by which he strove to guide his conduct. One rule in particular closely echoes the teaching of the Masters of the Far East: "You may be whatever you resolve to be." And "Old Jack," as young Tom was known to his friends, had resolved to be more than an ordinary West Pointer—he wanted to be a great soldier.

Jackson was a second lieutenant when he saw service in the artillery in the war with Mexico. He soon rose to first lieutenant and then, for his gallantry in action, was promoted to the rank of captain. There was no stopping this daring soldier, who placed his trust in himself and his God, and was indifferent to the enemy's fire. Within a year he was a major. His friends and his superiors esteemed him for his honesty, which knew no limits, his love of the truth, his fearlessness, and his straight-forwardness.

After the Mexican War, a long period of peace ensued. Jackson became a professor at the Virginia military institute, where for ten years he taught military science and other subjects. As he taught, he studied, too, widening his knowledge of the strategy and tactics of warfare. Although he was a soldier, he was not cast in any hell-and-brimstone mold; he was a deeply religious man and he lived his religion. He always showed great kindness to the slaves, teaching them the wisdom of the Bible.

In 1861, the North and the South arrived at the breaking point. Jackson could not forget the loyalty he owed his native Virginia, and offered his services to the South. He was made a colonel of infantry, and in a few months, a brigadier general.

Jackson knew that a general, no matter how brilliant, could never attempt more than his soldiers were willing to execute. He concentrated on the training of his men. So well did he prepare the soldiers under his command that when they faced the terrible fire of the Federal troops at Bull Run—when other units were taking to their heels—they stood firm. Because of their steadfastness under fire, he was forever after known as "Stonewall" Jackson.

In battle after battle, Jackson showed himself worthy of the trust the South placed in him. Self-assurance and success were rooted in the nature of his being. He is credited with the major part in stopping McClellan's deadly advance upon Richmond. Without him, it is probable that the Confederacy would have lost the Second Battle of Bull Run. General Robert E. Lee called him his good right arm. Jackson was dreaded by the Federal Armies as much as any man alive.

Where all the planning and courage of the enemy had failed to harm the dauntless Stonewall Jackson, the stupidity of people on his own side succeeded. After his greatest victory, in the Wilderness, near Chancellorsville, he met his death through an accident. Inspecting enemy positions after dark, he and his officers were mistaken for Northerners by the Confederate sentries, who opened fire, wounding him fatally.

If you travel through the South, you will see several fine statues erected to Jackson's memory. None is more meaningful than the one at Richmond. The first contribution toward its cost came from the Baptist congregation of Negro slaves to which he had shown so much kindness in his days at the military institute in Virginia.

Just as he refused to accept the lot of a poor Southerner in a humble country town, Jackson refused to remain an ordinary shavetail, serving his time till he was eligible for a pension. Thought is character, and the thoughts of this singular man were high ones. His lofty, ambitious thoughts won him not only worldly success, but a permanent niche in the pantheon of military greatness.

THOUGHTS CONTROL ACTIONS

Among the Masters of the Far East, thoughts are recognized as having so profound an influence on one's life that they are conceived of, literally, as being "things." The Masters say that thoughts have an actual existence—they are practically alive, for they possess reality in space, have a certain form, move at different rates of speed, and last for certain periods of time.

Thoughts have the power to control actions. If you are the master of your thoughts, say the Masters, you can make them do your bidding and be a powerful help to you; but if you do not direct them, they will direct you, ensnare you, and lead you to misfortune. Listen to the words of Buddha, the Enlightened One, set down by him in the *Dhammapada:*

"As the shaper of arrows makes straight his arrow, a wise man makes straight his trembling and unsteady thought, which is difficult to guard, difficult to hold back.

"As a fish taken from his watery home and thrown on the dry ground, our thought trembles all over in order to escape the dominion of Mara, the Tempter.

"It is good to tame the mind, which is often difficult to hold in and flighty, rushing wherever it listeth; a tamed mind brings happiness.

"Let the wise man guard his thoughts, for they are difficult to perceive, very artful, and they rush wherever they list: thoughts well guarded bring happiness."

Aim Your Thoughts Well

Buddha's advice, though exceedingly ancient, has not diminished in value with the passing of time. If you wish to improve your circumstances, mold your thoughts firmly and surely and always keep them in your control. If you let your thoughts arise as they will, and fly forth at random, you will never hit the target you have set for yourself in life.

Without thought direction, there is little chance of success. One of America's most distinguished poets, a contemporary of Stonewall Jackson's, was Henry Wadsworth Longfellow; countless millions have been enthralled by his masterpieces *The Courtship of Miles Standish, Evangeline,* and *Hiawatha.* Longfellow did not achieve greatness, any more than Stonewall Jackson did, simply by thinking of it now and then; his mind dwelled upon it all the time. As he said: "I most eagerly aspire after future eminence in literature; my whole soul burns most ardently for it, and every earthly thought centers in it." Longfellow kept his thoughts constantly aimed at his target. That is how he won fame and immortality.

Compare Henry Wadsworth Longfellow to the thousands of minor poets whom hardly anyone outside their own circles has ever heard of; or to the still more thousands of would-be poets who have played with the idea of writing verse but have never gotten around to putting their thoughts on paper. The reason they cannot succeed as Longfellow did is that they allow their thoughts to escape them as they arise. Thoughts have a life of their own, and unless you make them do what you want them to do, they will go their own way, futile shots from your bow.

THE POVERTY THOUGHT

An incredible number of thoughts arise in your mind every day. Many have an enormous power to do you harm, just as an arrow accidentally shot from a bow may kill or wound. One of these injurious thoughts is the poverty thought.

If you come of a poor family, the poverty thought is almost your natural heritage. From childhood days onward, you became accustomed to thinking that all your years must be lean ones. You take it for granted that you cannot rise above your circumstances. Perhaps your father was a humble man before you, and you suppose your lot can be no better than his was. The poverty thought paralyzes you, making you incapable of liberating the great energies that lie dormant within you.

Many people who are poor will tell you that they want little enough out of life. They are ready to be contented with a small income and modest circumstances. Since the thought is the ancestor of the deed, they do not aspire very high. The inevitable result is that they do not achieve very much. The man or woman who wants success must counter the poverty thought with the wealth thought. How this may be done will be explained later when we consider the Method of Contrary Concentration.

THE FAILURE THOUGHT

Another arrow that deals death to the ambition of innumerable human beings is the failure thought. Often it strikes us in childhood, just as the poverty thought does.

When we were children, we possessed a strong desire to do things for ourselves. The first time we managed to put our own socks on, or tied our shoelaces, we felt as proud of our achievement as Stonewall Jackson did when he won an important battle, or Longfellow when he finished a great poem. When for the first time we set the table or put our room to rights by ourselves we felt a glow of satisfaction perhaps as warm as any that life has to offer.

Experts in child psychology nowadays advise that parents who want to prepare their children for successful adulthood should praise them when they do a thing well. The experts remind us that a sense of achievement in small things inspires us with the confidence we need in order to attempt and accomplish great things. Experience teaches us the accuracy of this observation. But how many of us are open-minded enough to learn from experience?

Often, parents see only a child's shortcomings. The youngster, holding up a drawing on which he has lavished much labor, may say, "Look, Mother, isn't it a nice clown I've drawn?" And the mother, looking at the child's picture with the eyes of an adult, shakes her head and replies, "It doesn't look much like a clown to me." Or else, because in setting the table the child has misplaced a fork or a spoon, she scolds him for his error, completely overlooking the things he has done correctly. If she behaves this way repeatedly, the child begins to believe that he cannot do anything well or successfully. The seed of the failure thought, planted and watered by the parent's ignorance, can grow into a monstrous weed that will choke a child's confidence in himself forever.

Employers, too, often have very little understanding of the pervasive importance of the failure thought in keeping a person from doing his best. Many a time a new employee will do a job as best he can, yet when the boss looks at it he will see its shortcomings only. He will emphasize to the worker what is wrong, without giving a thought to the fact that on the whole the job is well done. Should this happen again and again, the employee will lose confidence in his ability to do what is expected of him. The failure thought takes control of his mind. The almost inevitable result is that he will quit, or else the quality of his performance will deteriorate and he will be discharged, to go off in search of new employment with his sense of self-esteem seriously damaged.

THE SICKNESS THOUGHT

Perhaps nowhere will you find more marked evidence of the power of thought to help or to harm than in the sphere of health. There are millions of people in the world today who are crippled by the sickness thought. Although the germ of their disease is mental, these persons are actually physically ill, with the concrete, recognizable symptoms of specific maladies. They complain of headaches, insomnia, susceptibility to colds, and a host of other common ailments. Others may show signs of graver disturbances. All of these illnesses are on occasion caused by sickness thoughts.

Is this hard to believe? Well, modern physicians believe it, although a generation ago most contended that disease had to have a physical cause. In the last few decades an entirely new viewpoint and a new branch of medicine have come into existence. It is known as Psychosomatic Medicine ("psychosomatic" is derived from the Greek words for "soul" and "body"), and this new study treats of diseases produced by the influence of the mind on the body, and the body on the mind.

The reason this branch of medicine was so slow in arising—and millions had to suffer because of erroneous diagnosis and consequent incorrect treatment—is that the West has been accustomed for ages to think of the mind and body as separate and independent entities. In this field, as in others, it required true genius to discover a fact that should have been obvious from the start: that the mind is a function of the brain, which is a part of the body, and therefore influences it greatly and is in turn influenced by it.

Only a moment's reflection will suffice to prove the soundness of the mind-body view of illness. When you are bored or dispirited, you frequently find you have a headache, too, or else you are overcome by a feeling of fatigue, although you have not engaged in physical effort. Your state of mind infects your body. If something disturbing happens, you "feel sick to your stomach," and cannot eat. If you are physically unwell, you fall prey to a fit of depression and are frequently unable to concentrate.

FAITH CURES

The Masters of the Far East attained an understanding of the mind-body relationship thousands of years ago. As we saw earlier, they recognized the fundamental unity of all things, which they called "Brahma," and taught that we cannot separate the action of the mind from the body. Christian Science also discovered this truth for itself long before most physicians did. It is the secret of Christ's healing. Once Jesus removed the sickness thought from a person, that man became whole again. The cures performed by other great religious leaders and holy men are made on the same basis. This is the scientific explanation of the miracles at Lourdes, where, with the help of faith, sick persons make themselves well again.

Oriental physicians, having a knowledge of the teaching of the Masters of the Far East, have since ancient times considered the close connection between sickness and states of the mind or emotions, in making a diagnosis. Where an illness is not overtly physical in origin, they immediately turn their attention to the patients' feelings. Like the Masters, they have always maintained that by making one's thoughts and desires pure, one could control his general health, provided simple hygienic measures were taken.

How Emotions Influence the Body

The precise mechanisms by which the emotions influence the body are complicated, but some are well known today. Strong feelings send messages along the pathways of the nerves to the endocrine glands, stimulating them to produce hormones. These hormones, sometimes known as "chemical messengers," travel through the blood stream, stimulating the heart, the stomach, and other organs to greater or lesser activity. Like almost every other part of the body, the chemical messengers are important to our physical well-being. But if our emotions are constantly telegraphing alarms to the glands, and these are made over-active, the result is not a happy one.

Fear and anger are among the most dangerous of the emotions. When you are angry, the anger thought produces a profound effect throughout the body. For one thing, the stomach is stimulated to secrete large amounts of hydrochloric acid, a powerful chemical. If this happens often enough, you may suffer from chronic indigestion or worse disorders.

Physicians and scientists have had ample opportunity to look directly into the stomach of a man and observe how it is affected by his emotions. A noted case is that of a man named Tom, who has been studied by Dr. Harold G. Wolff and his colleagues at Cornell

University. When Tom was a boy, he had to have an emergency operation, which left an opening in his stomach. Peering through this "hole" today, the doctors can see how Tom feels about the things that are in his mind.

For example, on one occasion, one of the physicians told Tom that he was not doing a good job and that he would be discharged. (This of course was a trick to provoke a reaction.) Tom felt what the doctor had said was very unfair; he became furious, and his face turned red. He complained bitterly to Dr. Wolff when the physician had left.

Immediately afterward, Dr. Wolff looked into Tom's stomach. He saw that it had become a bright red and that the stomach glands were pouring hydrochloric acid into it. He observed a large number of minute hemorrhages in the stomach wall, and that the stomach was expanding and contracting at a furious rate. It is in much the same way as this, when people are subjected to continuous worry and stress, that stomach ulcers are produced.

THE FEAR THOUGHT AND ILLNESS

A man becomes what he thinks—including what he fears, if the fears are strong and persistent. Many sickness thoughts have their origin in fear. For confirmation of this we may look at one curious ailment, which goes by the formidable name of "iatrogenic heart disease." Like so many other disorders, this one is particularly common in the overemotional—those who have never learned to understand and control their thoughts and feelings. "Iatrogenic" means, literally, "produced by a physician." That's an odd term, but physicians make use of it. It describes the following sort of case:

A man goes to a doctor for a physical examination. The doctor scrutinizes his visitor's anatomy, takes his blood pressure, and applies the stethoscope to his chest. What does he hear? Generally, the sound of a normal heart. However, the doctor is an earnest, hard-working person, and he frowns as he concentrates on the sound; many of us knit our brows when we concentrate. To the patient, however, the doctor's frown immediately suggests the thought that there is something seriously the matter with his heart. He asks the doctor, who assures him he is quite all right. Still the doctor, possibly because he lacks a bedside manner, does not smile. The patient, whose mind is ever open to sickness thoughts, now supposes the doctor is lying, because he does not want to tell him the "dreadful truth." He goes from physician to physician, trying to find one who will confirm his worst fears. He worries endlessly. His digestion is disturbed, he cannot sleep, and his tension reflects itself in a rise in his blood pressure. In time, the constant worry and strain may wear down his heart, producing the very trouble that he feared.

Paralyzed by Fear

Where fears are heightened, there you will find the most dreadful examples of the influence of the emotions on the body. Our two world wars have provided harrowing proof of the truth of the psychosomatic concept. Under the stress of war, soldiers have lost the power to use their limbs, the ability to see and speak—all without direct physical injury. In time, sympathetic treament and analysis of their fears and other personal problems have brought many of them around. These are the illnesses that used to be known as "shell shock"; the term has now passed out of use, since many of its worst casualties occurred far from the field of battle.

The emotion of fear not only maims people—it kills them as well. One of the gravest dangers to any person who has been injured is shock. A man may be knocked down by an automobile, or fall from a first-story window and die immediately. When he is examined, it is not unusual for the physician to find that the loss of blood or the extent of the injury suffered was insufficient to cause death. The patient died because his fear and the jolt to his nervous system were so great that his heart stopped. In all cases of serious injury, first aid procedure recommends that the patient be treated for shock, which may be the gravest danger to which he has been exposed.

We can find many curious examples of the power of thought to create a physical reaction. One of the most interesting is related by the scientist Count Alfred Korzybski. He tells of a man who was allergic to roses. So fearful to this man was the sight of roses that when, on one occasion, he was shown a picture of these flowers, he was seized by a powerful attack of sneezing.

More than half of all hospital beds in the United States are occupied by persons suffering from mental illness. Although this type of disturbance arises in the mind, it is not imaginary. As we have seen, thoughts are mighty things for good or evil.

We have seen that, for good or ill, thought is the greatest force on earth. In the larger sphere, it has been responsible for the progress and civilization whose fruits we enjoy today. The helpful inventions of an Edison or of a Wilbur or Orville Wright, the life-saving discoveries of a Pasteur, the literary creations of a Longfellow—all are the products of good thinking. The collective, constructive thinking of scores of wise men imaged forth the shape and plan of our great democratic country before it could be made into reality.

In the smaller, personal sphere, we have seen that thought influences every atom of our being, and can make us healthy or make us ill. It can help us to remold our circumstances in the image of our most cherished desires—or it can keep us mired in a slough of poverty, failure, and despair. We can no longer question the truth of the words of Bodhidharma, the Master Yogin of China, who said: "There is neither cause nor effect apart from the mind and heart. Nirvana itself is a state of the heart."

Whether you are rich or poor, well or ill, cheerful or dispirited, is very much up to yourself. All human experience proclaims that tomorrow need not be like today. Life, the Masters tell us, is infinitely plastic and malleable. If you take it firmly and knowingly in your hands in the way of the Masters—and their way is not a difficult one—you can refashion it as you would like it to be. But if you work blindly and without forethought, you may make of it a nightmarish thing.

"You will be what you will to be;
    Let failure find its false content
    In that poor word "environment,"
But spirit scorns it, and is free.

"It masters time, it conquers space;
    It cows that boastful trickster, Chance,
    And bids the tyrant Circumstance
Uncrown, and fill a servant's space.

"The human Will, that force unseen,
    The offspring of a deathless Soul,
    Can hew a way to any goal,
Though walls of granite intervene.

"Be not impatient in delay,
    But wait as one who understands;
    When spirit rises and commands,
The gods are ready to obey."

CHAPTER IV

DHARANA—METHOD
OF THE MASTERS

"A man becomes what he thinks," says an Upanishad *mantra*. Experience of wise men testifies to the truth of the aphorism."

MAHATMA GANDHI

What is it that makes some people great and others small? Why do the few succeed and the many fail? The Masters of the Far East knew the secret. They summed it up in one word: *dharana*. It represents no mystic law, but plain, undiluted common sense. We behold the effectiveness of *dharana* in the life of every man or woman who achieves anything substantial.

FROM HUMBLE BEGINNINGS

One of the greatest captains of industry the world has ever known was Andrew Carnegie. He reaped a fortune in the iron and steel industries. He prospered to such an extent that he was able to give away $56,000,000 to establish public libraries—300 millions more to found universities and to establish charities—and still have millions left. Yet, had you

observed this tycoon as a youth, you would probably not have been impressed. At age twelve he was
working as a "bobbin boy" in a cotton factory in
Allegheny City, Pennsylvania, for the magnificent
wage of $1.20 a week.

Still, young Carnegie had something that most of
us do not—an intuitive understanding of the meaning
of *dharana*.

Andrew Carnegie recognized very early that his
job at the cotton factory would get him nowhere. He
might have complained that he had to be at work
before sunrise, had less than an hour for lunch, and
his working day did not end before the sun went to
rest. But none of these hardships dismayed him. What
did bother him, though, was the knowledge that the
factory afforded him scant opportunity to better himself. In young Carnegie, ambition was not a flame
that flickered, but an all-consuming blaze.

WHERE THERE'S A WILL

After a few years in the factory, he went to Pittsburgh, and got a job as a messenger at the telegraph
office. Pittsburgh, then, was smaller than it is today,
but a messenger still had to know his way around.
Andrew went about the strange city and memorized
every important street in it, and the names of prominent individuals and business organizations that were
on each street. He got to know the addresses so well
that he could call them out, one after another, from
the start of each street to its end.

Young Carnegie had not been satisfied to remain
a bobbin boy; the job of messenger, likewise, was
not the summit of his ambitions. He wanted to go

further with the telegraph company, and the next job up the ladder was that of clerk and operator. But how could he get ahead if he did not know telegraphy? Nor did there seem to be a chance to learn it; the telegraph instrument was in use all day, and, besides, he had his messages to deliver.

Once he had made up his mind to become a telegrapher, Andrew began to come to work earlier. He arrived so early that the telegrapher was not in yet. Sitting down at the instrument, Andrew would practice the Morse code. Day after day he practiced, until he could send it and receive it flawlessly. He came to know the code so well that he could take it by ear, without laboriously writing down the letters of each word until they formed a message.

One morning, as usual, Andrew Carnegie was in the office before the operator had arrived. The telegraph began to click out the code for "death message." Such messages were considered important and Andrew thought he ought to take that one. Now his early morning practice stood him in good stead. By the time the operator came in, not only had the boy taken the message perfectly—he had delivered it as well. After that, the operators accepted young Carnegie as one of themselves.

Young Carnegie Forges Ahead

This youth, as anyone could see, had something special in him. He was bound to excel at whatever task he turned his hand to. His ability was quickly recognized by T. A. Scott, of the Pennsylvania Railroad. Scott engaged him as his secretary. At his new job, the boy showed the same remarkable qualities as before, which the Hindus would describe as *dharana*. When Scott became vice president of the railway, Andrew, then in his early twenties, was made superintendent of the western section of the line.

Andrew Carnegie was not ready to rest upon his laurels, even though he had accomplished more than most men do in a lifetime. He studied the railway, looked hard for ways to improve it, and found them. Before he was thirty, he had been responsible for introducing sleeping cars on American railways, and was already a wealthy man. He saved his money, and when he saw an opportunity to make a sound investment in oil wells that were just crying to be exploited, he did so. His greatest achievements still lay before him, however, in the development of the iron and steel industry. When he retired from business, his interests were worth not much less than half a billion dollars.

Is that a lot of money? Do you think the achievments of a Carnegie are beyond your powers? No, what one has done, others may do, if they but know the secret of achievement, *dharana,* or concentration.

What Is This Thing Called Luck?

"Just a moment," you may be thinking. "There's one thing you have overlooked. "Andrew Carnegie had luck, too. He came at the right time. America was moving into an age of railways, of oil, iron, and steel. Carnegie just had the good fortune to see it. He bet on the right horses. I wish I had his luck."

But what, after all, is this thing called luck? By it do you mean a fortunate accident?

Of course a man may profit considerably by a fortunate accident. But strokes of fortune are few and far between. Some people do bet on a horse or buy a ticket in the sweepstakes and win—but how often does it happen to a given person? Ask any regular bettor and he will tell you—with a sad shake of his head—not often.

Dame Fortune, we say, is fickle. This means simply that fortunate accidents don't go on happening to the same person.

In ancient Rome, Fortune was revered as a goddess; but when the Romans engaged in a war, they sent forth the most thoroughly trained soldiery in the world, armed with the most up-to-date, effective weapons known, and under the command of generals with brilliant records of success in warfare. The Romans worshipped Fortune, but they depended on themselves.

Not Enough Brains?

"All very well and good," you may say. "So there is no Dame Fortune. So it wasn't luck that made Carnegie great. But he certainly was a sharp-witted fellow. I guess I just don't have the brains that he had."

But don't you? That is precisely the question.

Roughly speaking each of us has the same quantity of brains as a so-called "genius." Science tells us that it isn't even the quantity of our brains that counts.

No, the difference between the ordinary man and the Carnegie, the Shakespeare, or the Lincoln is not that the last three possess more brains. They did not inherit superior brain power, which automatically destined them for a higher position in life. Their fathers, and their fathers' fathers, were born humble folk and remained humble folk. The insignificance of the hereditary factor can be proved by looking forward as well as back. We do not possess a single immortal line written by Shakespeare's parents or his children, though Shakespeare himself was the greatest master of language that ever took pen in hand. Both the ancestors and the descendants of Carnegie and Lincoln failed to make an imposing name for themselves. The heirs of our self-made millionaires are better known for the way they spend their fathers' hard-earned fortunes than for the new fortunes they accumulate through their own efforts.

In the final analysis, the secret of getting ahead in life does not lie in the breaks or the brains. It lies in what the Hindu sages call *dharana* or concentration —in making the most of the mental ability you were born with. The sages tell us that the average man uses only a minute fraction of his God-given powers. Having only the remotest conception of what his mind is and how it works, he fails to bring into play what is the greatest force on earth.

A JEST OF HISTORY

It is one of the jests of history that the science of the mind has been the last of the sciences to be discovered. Although it is primarily his mind that makes man superior to brute creation—that has enabled him to create wonders surpassing even those found in nature—man seldom thinks about his mind and never employs it to its fullest capacity.

Four thousand years ago, the Egyptians had an advanced understanding of architecture, navigation, the science of measurement. Twenty-five hundred years ago, the Greeks were studying the heavens and already had a more-than-fair comprehension of the principles of astronomy. The ancient Romans, two thousand years back, were masters of medicine, engineering, warfare, literature, and philosophy. Yet these distinguished peoples of antiquity, for all their momentous achievements and knowledge, rarely gave a thought to thought itself!

The science of the mind, which we call psychology, only began to get its footing in the West about sixty years ago, when the first psychological laboratory was set up in Europe. That science, though its contributions are already impressive, is still in its infancy.

SCIENCE OF THE YOGIS

It may be an oddity, but it certainly is no accident that the Masters of the Orient anticipated many of the great modern psychological discoveries of the Western world. The yogis, we have seen, were masters of mental power thousands of years ago. They had to be, for control over the feelings and thought processes—the development of will power—is the first step toward the achievement of yoga. As Patanjali expresses it in one of his opening sutras: "Yoga is achieved by developing full mastery over the mind and emotions." This mastery is attained through what the sages call *dharana*. It implies the ability to bend your mind and will to a purpose until you have achieved it. As part of the process, you learn how to use the untapped reserves of your subconscious mind.

THE SUBCONSCIOUS MIND

What is the Subconscious Mind? Most people are completely unaware of the vast powers they carry about with them during all their lives. William James said that by ignoring these mighty forces, the average person uses only about 10% of his actual potential mental power. Think of it! Only 10%! He has almost unlimited power—yet ignores 90% of it. Unlimited wealth all about him—and he doesn't know how to take hold of it. With God-like powers slumbering within him, he is content to continue in his daily grind —eating, sleeping, working—plodding through a dull, routine existence. Yet all of Nature, all of life, calls upon him to awaken and bestir himself!

YOU ARE THE TRUE MASTER OF YOUR DESTINY

The POWER to be whatever you want to be, to get what you want in life, to accomplish whatever you are striving for, lies dormant, sleeping within you until you call upon it. You need only bring it forth and put it to work. True, you must learn HOW to do that. But the first essential is to realize and believe that you DO possess this power; the first objective must be to get acquainted with it—get the "feel" of it.

Psychologists and Metaphysicians the world over agree on this: that the MIND is all that counts. You can be whatever you make up your mind to be. You need not be sick. You need not be unhappy. You need not be unsuccessful. You are not a mere clod on this earth. You are not a beast of burden, doomed to spend your days in drudgery, just eking out a bare existence.

You are one of the Lords of the Earth, with unlimited potentialities. Within you is a power which, properly grasped and directed, can lift you out of the rut of mediocrity and place you among the Elect of the earth—the DOERS, the THINKERS, the LEADERS among men. It rests with you and you only to use this power which is your neglected heritage— this MIND which can do all things!

How *NOT* to Solve Problems

The average person solves his problems with the aid of his conscious mind only and many times this leads him to make a complete mess of his life. When he is confronted with a problem, his conscious mind comes up with a hundred solutions. The conscious mind is very willing to give its opinions, based on past experiences, hearsay, superstition, inclinations to be lazy, etc. And let's not overlook another factor that influences a person's decisions—his worry about what other people will say or think as a result of his actions. He must abide by man-made conventions, customs, mores, and mortal beliefs; however erroneous they may be.

The more so-called intelligence people may have, the more and bigger mistakes they are likely to make through planning guided solely by the conscious mind. Just look at the colossal blunders made by our best brains in the treaties and pacts drafted during and after World War Two. They unwittingly helped to make Communism one of the biggest world powers and a threat to our very existence. Look at the corruption and stupid planning in many local and national governments today—all the result of mortal planning by the conscious minds of so-called leaders of men.

Let Your Sub-Conscious Mind Plan Your Life

Most people entirely neglect a mighty source of information, guidance, and inspiration, in overlooking the slumbering giant within them—the subconscious mind.

By consciously instructing your Inner Mind to solve the questions and dilemmas that come into your life, you can relieve your conscious mind of 90% of its worry and mental deliberations and speculations. You can avoid having to ponder over, cudgel or ransack your brains, for the answer to every predicament that clouds your path.

You can easily acquire the habit of forming in your mind the question to be answered, or the problem to be solved, so that you know what you wish accomplished, and just upon what subject you wish to be informed. Then you can intentionally turn over the problem to your Inner or subconscious mind, who will at once analyze it and separate it into its elements or integrant parts; then proceed to solve, decipher, and untangle the problem.

In this way the subconscious mind can relieve you of much of the drudgery of thought; thus allowing your conscious mind to occupy itself busily and efficiently with other tasks, while important solutions are prepared for your revelation underneath the surface of consciousness.

The Miracle of Memory

The action of the subconscious mind is called upon by us every day in countless ways, but perhaps most frequently for the purpose of remembering. Everyone has had the experience of trying to recall a name that used to be familiar but has now slipped from consciousness. Sometimes it seems to be almost on the tip of your tongue—yet when you say it, it does not sound quite right. So you give up. Then, a few hours later, almost miraculously, the name comes back to you clear and exact, together with many facts associated with it.

The subconscious mind, you see, is not only a thinking machine—it is also the storehouse of memory. Filed away in it, in orderly fashion, are all the things that have ever happened to you, everything you have ever known. Figuratively speaking, it contains hundreds of rooms with filing cabinets, packed with millions of details that have been a part of your experience. Even when you have consciously given up the search for the detail you wanted to remember, the subconscious goes on seeking, trying one filing cabinet after the other until it has found the answer.

You can develop a wonderfully efficient memory-machine. The memory never really loses or forgets anything once placed in it properly. Remembrance and recollection depend chiefly upon proper methods of indexing and cross-indexing subjects in your brain.

The True Psychic Reality

How much of the mind is conscious, how much subconscious? Scientific investigations conducted over the past seventy-five years leave little doubt about the pre-eminence of our subconscious faculties.

Dr. Sigmund Freud, often called the father of psychoanalysis, has said, "the unconscious (subconscious) must be accepted as the general basis of the psychic life. The unconscious is the larger circle which includes the smaller circle of the conscious; everything conscious has a preliminary unconscious stage . . . the unconscious is the true psychic reality."

INSPIRATION FROM THE SUBCONSCIOUS

In all mental activity, we observe the subconscious mind playing a paramount role. Its influence is held to be most marked in creative matters, where the results of its action are known as "inspiration." The inventor who suddenly stumbles upon the means of perfecting his invention, the manufacturer who by chance discovers the way to sell a previously unmarketable product, the poet who suddenly comes upon the right words to use in his poem, the scientist who accidentally hits upon the long-sought-for ingredient needed to complete his formula, all praise their inspiration—which is in reality nothing more nor less than the product of subconscious thinking.

Dr. Freud, who devoted a lifetime to the study of the subconscious, has put it this way: "We are probably much too inclined to overestimate the conscious character even of intellectual and artistic production. From the reports of certain writers who have been highly productive, such as Goethe and Helmholtz, we learn rather that the most essential and original part of their creations came to them in the form of inspirations, and offered itself to their awareness in an almost completed state."

It is clear, then, that the subconscious mind is the dynamo of ideas that supplies men in all walks of life with the swift flow of inspiration that they need for success. Correctly managed, it is a source of incredible power that can make you one of the mighty ones of the earth. If you learn how to employ it wisely, you will never want for ideas and the energy you need to see them through.

How can you learn to make the most of your subconscious mind—that mighty force, next to which your conscious mind is the puniest of pygmies? The answer is: through mastery of the art of concentration, which the Masters of the Far East call *dharana*.

Some have achieved great things without any knowledge of the method of the Masters. Andrew Carnegie probably never even heard of it; yet intuitively he grasped its principles. It is probable that Stonewall Jackson had only the faintest inkling of the teachings of the Orient. But he knew them unconsciously, for his words echo those of the Masters. Great men have an almost instinctive understanding of the inner principles of life.

The rest of us, however, without guidance, are doomed to spend our lives groping in darkness. Because we cannot see well, we waste years wandering back and forth in blind alleys, when we could be walking straight up the broad highway to success. Within ourselves we feel the instinct for greatness, but we do not know how to bring it forth.

*   *   *

70

All of this is by way of a preface. It demonstrates the scientific basis on which the wisdom of the Orient is founded. In the next chapter you will see that wisdom in action. You will learn how to make your efforts as fruitful as those of any man or woman alive. The method of the Masters, with its easily understood principles, will show you the way to unleash the power of your subconscious mind so that it will carry you straight to your heart's desire.

So concrete and productive is this method, that it will bring you quick results if you follow it only briefly. If you adhere to it firmly and persistently, no man can tell how far you may go.

CHAPTER V

THE FIRST SECRET

If the will knows not what to will, it will not be able
to will.

—LAO-TZE

New York City has one of the greatest harbors on
earth. In fair weather or foul, every day dozens of
ships make their way toward this vast port. Some are
small vessels from nearby points. Others are huge
ocean liners and freight carriers that come from the
far corners of the earth—Hongkong, Macao, Bombay,
or Capetown. Whether from near or far, however, all
these ships have one thing in common—they know
where they are going.

Suppose the captain of one of these ships, before
he left his home port, opened his sailing orders and
found that they failed to name the ship's destination.
He might have the finest vessel that ever put to sea
and a crew of superb sailors—but he never could reach
the end of his voyage, could he? Even if he cast anchor
at the right port, he would quickly sail out again without unloading his cargo; not having any idea of his
goal, how could he tell he had reached it?

Of course no captain in his right mind would ever

put to sea without explicit sailing orders. Yet millions of people do just that. They set out in life with the hope of getting somewhere, yet never bother to determine the place they want to get to. If, as generally happens, they never arrive anywhere, they have only themselves to blame.

Most of humanity drift with the tides, letting the ebb and flow of life take them where it will. They are living flotsam and jetsam; lacking resolve and direction, they frequently find themselves cast up on unfriendly, barren shores.

Others do have goals, but they keep shifting them, which is almost as bad. We call such people dilettantes. It may happen that they are quite intelligent and talented. Their major shortcoming is that they have never decided what use they wish to make of their talents. So they fritter them away, with a thriftlessness that amounts to folly.

Don't Be a Dilettante

Every one of us knows people of this type. I can think, for example, of an old friend of my own, who is one of the most likable people you could wish to know. Here I will refer to him as Tom, though that is not his real name.

Each year, Tom discovers a new enterprise in which he feels he will make his fortune. After a number of months he loses heart and gives it up.

At one time, Tom was going to be an inventor. He studied many successful inventions with the thought of finding some patentable improvement he could make on them. When the going began to get tough, he decided this was not the career for him.

73

Tom had many hobbies. One of them was amateur photography. Casting about for a new goal, he was impressed by the success of outstanding professional photographers like Margaret Bourke-White and Robert Capa. He decided he would become an artistic photographer and give them a run for their money.

So Tom set out to take photographs on a big scale. Wherever he went, he carried his camera with him. He took candid shots of children sitting at windows, he snapped pictures of old cathedral spires, and of broken-down shanties.

When he showed his photographs to me, it seemed to me that some were very good, but many were quite mediocre. It was my considered opinion that if he would work at his photography, after a suitable period of apprenticeship he would probably be capable of doing excellent things.

However, Tom is not the patient type. He offered the pictures to a few magazines; they manifested moderate interest, but were not ready to buy any. Disheartened, he decided that he wasn't cut out to be a photographer. Now he looked about for greener pastures.

Tom's next resolution was to become an artist. He bought himself easel, paints, and canvases, and started to paint like a demon. His first pictures were crude, but they did show promise. (I have said that he is a talented person.) Before long, he was selling some. As months went by, his style improved. But by now he was no longer sure he wanted to be a painter. The rewards were not precisely what he had expected they would be, and he already had an itch to try his hand at writing fiction.

Since then, Tom has passed through five additional careers and is now looking for a new one. No doubt he's had a lot of fun—but he's haunted by a sense of never having found himself. His wife, after fifteen years of marriage, still does not know where her next week's household money is coming from.

Contrast Tom with the type of man who decides early in life just what he wants to do, and then puts all of his heart and soul into doing it. Compare him to Andrew Carnegie or Stonewall Jackson. Wolfgang Amadeus Mozart provides us with an extraordinary one.

He Knew What He Wanted

Mozart was probably the greatest musical prodigy that ever lived. Although he has been dead for over one hundred and fifty years, thousands and thousands of recordings and printed copies of his music are sold every month. In the great cities of the world, like London, Paris, Rome, and Leipzig, every year the finest musical artists present his masterpieces to applauding audiences. Children study his simpler compositions when they learn to play the piano or violin. Yet the life work of this great genius was finished when, only thirty-six years old, he was stricken by typhus.

How did Mozart achieve so much in so little time? A clue to the answer is found in the remarkable fact that he knew *when he was only three years old* that he wanted to be a musician. He came of a musical family; not only did he, like so many children, want to follow in his father's footsteps, but he never swerved from that decision. Because he knew his aim in life, not an ounce of his energy was wasted. At nine, he was writing sonatas as good as any that experienced musicians were producing. In his twenties, he composed great operas—*The Marriage of Figaro, The Magic Flute, Cosi Fan Tutte*—each in a few months of intense effort. He died at an age when most men are just discovering their mature powers—yet no composer before or since has ever surpassed him. (The official catalogue of his works comprises 626 compositions, including twenty-two operas!)

If, like Mozart, you know what you want out of life, half of the battle for success is won. You do not waste precious months and years. Like an arrow well aimed, your ambition will fly directly to the bull's eye. As Oveta Culp Hobby said, "The knowledge of having chosen . . . an ultimate objective gives direction and emphasis to the days of one's years."

So, initially, before you can commence *dharana,* or concentration, you must decide just what you are going to concentrate *on*. Is it wealth or fame in the arts? Is it social success? If your sights are set on money, in which field do you wish to attain it? Your choice must be clear and definite; if you shift it from year to year, your fate will be that of the dilettante.

Consider Your Personality

In reaching a firm decision, you must consider your likes and dislikes and your aptitudes. Any goals you set for yourself should be in fundamental conformity with your personality. A salesman's commission may look highly attractive to you, but if you are a shy, introverted person, and feel ill at ease with people, you'd probably better find some other way to make money. If you hate details or haggling, you'd better not decide to become a manufacturer, for the man who buys and sells and makes things must pay close attention to costs and to a thousand and one details. If you enjoy society and cannot bear solitude, it might be a mistake to think of becoming a writer.

Experience shows that people do best the things they like best. People are most successful in jobs that hold a fundamental interest for them. Because they are interested, they find everything about their work appealing; what is labor to others is a lark to them.

We observe this principle very clearly in the performance of children in school. Some children take very readily to English, for example. They spell well, and can express their thoughts fluently and vividly. They get good grades in the subject simply because they enjoy working with language. Other children never seem to be able to get more than a passing grade, and they are always poor spellers. So strongly do some things appeal to people, and therefore so easy do these subjects become for them, that we almost suppose their skill to be congenital; we refer to one person as a "born businessman," to another as a "born salesman" or a "born musician."

Anyone can discover what is the best and most suitable objective for him to concentrate on. If there is a choice of several goals, choose the one that is most congenial for you on all counts. It may not at first offer as good remuneration as some other goal, but appearances are notoriously deceptive. If you choose the right goal for you, your interest will release your subconscious powers. It will call forth so much effortless energy and inspired activity that your earnings may soon be greater than those of friends engaged in what at the start appeared to be more profitable careers. Woodrow Wilson, speaking from long experience, once declared, "Enthusiasm comes with the revelation of true and satisfying objectives of devotion; and it is enthusiasm that sets the powers free."

Visualize Your Goals Concretely

Up to now we have been speaking in generalities. When we spoke of desirable goals to concentrate on, we described them as "wealth," or "success" or the like. Generalities have one peculiarity, however—they don't really exist.

To be more specific, a man doesn't look at his bank book and see "wealth" written there. What he sees is a balance of $500 or $5,000, or $50,000. "Success" likewise has no physical existence. But a man may own a fifteen-room house, have a brand-new Cadillac, 1,000 shares of A.T.&T., and be greeted with respect by everyone who knows him. That is the physical reality of success.

The first step of *dharana* is to visualize your goal concretely. Generalities, by their nature, lack substance. Vague goals are not very compelling. You can call forth your subconscious powers much more effectively if you offer them concrete rather than abstract objectives. Once you have something definite in mind, you can more readily go about achieving it.

How a Clear Understanding Helps

Suppose, for example, you decide that you want a new car. Unfortunately, however, you have not quite made up your mind whether it should be a Ford, a

78

Chrysler, a Pontiac, or some other make. Each has certain good or bad points from your point of view.

The likelihood is that you will spend your time reading through newspaper and magazine ads, or visiting automobile dealers' showrooms. When you see a Chrysler that looks fairly attractive to you, you will say to yourself: "Yes, it's nice, but a Pontiac (or a Ford or a Chevrolet) costs less." When you see an appealing Ford or Chevrolet, you may be tempted to buy, but then be held back by the thought: "A Pontiac or a Chrysler is sturdier—and there's more prestige in having one. I think I'll wait a while till I can afford one." Lack of a clear understanding of what we want accounts for much of the indecision and inaction in the world.

A clear-cut picture of the goal, on the other hand, is a call to immediate action.

Suppose you do decide that you want a brand-new Pontiac. Perhaps you still don't have enough money to buy it. But you know what you want. Every time you see a new Pontiac, it is a gleaming reminder of your objective. It summons you to save your money faster, or to go to the credit department of your bank for a loan, or to work harder for a raise. The fact is that one buys Pontiacs and Chevrolets and Chryslers, never a car on the abstract level. The sooner you know exactly what you want, the quicker will you get it.

POWER OF CONCRETE OBJECTS

That concrete objects call forth a stronger response from the depths of our minds may be proved in countless other ways. If you are like most human beings,

79

when someone speaks to you of the wretchedness of the poverty-stricken population of Korea, you will agree sadly that something should be done about it, and let the matter rest there. However, if you are shown a photograph of small Korean children with spindly legs, emaciated bodies, and a look of woe on their faces, you will probably be so moved that your hand will go immediately to your pocket.

Many religions, realizing the effectiveness of the concrete image upon the subconscious mind, ages ago made statues of their gods to inspire their followers. They did not necessarily mean to suggest that a figure of stone or plaster was actually inhabited by a divine spirit—but so compelling is the physical image that people have always regarded religious statues with awe.

THE LAW OF IMMEDIATE GOALS

Long-range goals, concretely visualized, are important to us if we are to achieve anything impressive over the years. But in order to have long-range goals, we must first have short-range ones. Each big objective has many smaller ones within itself; as we achieve these minor goals, the major ones begin to take form and reality.

This rule—we may call it the Law of Immediate Goals—provides the pattern for all sizable accomplishments. To see how it works, let's turn to an old story—a true story of how a band of Scotch soldiers won a remarkable victory.

The Scots were greatly outnumbered by their enemies, the Saracens. It seemed impossible for the Highlanders, valiant though they were, to break through the deep, spear-bristling lines of the foe. But the Scots had cut out the heart of Robert de Bruce, their dead leader, and it proved to be a magic talisman.

One of the soldiers held the heart up so that all could see. With a loud shout, he threw it forward, right into the enemy lines. Another shout, and the Scots were advancing into the midst of the enemy to recapture the strange missile. Moments of sharp hand-to-hand fighting followed, and then they had the heart in their hands once more.

But this was only the beginning. The soldier who had been lucky enough to regain the heart flung it again, this time still deeper into the ranks of the Saracens. Again the Scots surged forward, each man trying to be the first to get the heart. Thus they advanced, yard by yard, until finally they had broken through the Saracens and routed them. The great heart of Robert de Bruce, though it beat no more, had won the day for his countrymen.

What does this story teach? That you should make your goals really concrete by making them immediate —like the few yards the Scots had to push ahead each time to win back Bruce's heart. If, for example, you have set yourself the goal of acquiring wealth and security, don't visualize these as becoming yours at the end of two or three decades. Picture the amount of money you want to have at the end of each year. And don't just set the amount for the year; unless you put away some money week by week, you probably will never achieve the annual sum. Having decided on accumulating one thousand dollars in twelve months, you should determine how much you must put away each week to have that amount at the end of the year. Once you have decided precisely how much to save, you will be surprised at how easy it will be to save it.

Getting Ahead in Your Job

If your aim is to rise in your profession, don't be satisfied to picture yourself as earning five thousand dollars more a year at some date in the indefinite future. To get your subconscious powers to work for you now, you must offer them attractive bait—and in the immediate future. Say to yourself: "At the end of this year I will be getting a thousand dollars more than at present." Say it often. You will be astonished how soon opportunities will be presented to you—or found by your subconscious mind—to increase your value to the organization for which you work, and consequently your earning power, provided you faithfully apply the other simple rules of *dharana* expounded in this and the following chapters.

Extraordinary Sense Perceptions

In one of his most meaningful sutras, the Hindu sage Patanjali declares: "The kinds of concentration that produce extraordinary sense perceptions cause perseverance of the mind." In order to get a thing, it must first make a strong impression on your senses, which in turn make a powerful impression on your mind. The more powerful the impression, the more will every current in your subconscious be channeled to the achievement of your wish.

Immediate goals will make a strong impression on your senses—but how can you keep the impression so strong that your mind will really persevere through thick and thin till your wish is fulfilled?

You won't make a mistake if you take a hint from the old schoolroom where you learned the three R's. Probably you still remember some of the proverbs that your teacher had written on placards which she fastened up on the walls; perhaps your first knowledge of what George Washington looked like, or Abraham Lincoln, goes back to pictures you observed in that classroom. *Because you saw them every day, they stuck with you.*

Impressions on the Subconscious

Most of us are extremely visual minded. If we see something, we are likely to remember it much better than if we merely hear it. (Musicians and some others are an exception to this rule.) So it's bound to prove helpful, in visualizing our objectives concretely, if we don't see them merely with our mind's eye, but with our body's eyes as well. So to speak, we must reverse the old proverb: "Out of sight, out of mind."

How To Strengthen the Images

Let's get down to cases. What are the things you have set your heart on? Do you want a new car? Then clip a picture of the car you want, and put it in a place where you will see it often. Does a lovely new house appeal to you more? Hunt through the magazines for a house of the type you want and clip it out. Put these pictures of your concrete objectives in a folder

83

or paste them in a notebook and look at them regularly, perhaps every morning and evening. As you look at them, think how much you want them. Try as hard as you can to make a forceful impression upon your conscious mind. Your conscious mind will telegraph the image to your subconscious, and both will work together to achieve your aim for you.

GETTING THE THINGS YOU WANT

Utilize every means you can think of for strengthening the images of the things you want. Remember, the more sharply and the more often you visualize them, the quicker will you realize them.

Do you want financial security? Take out your bank book often and observe the way each deposit makes your savings grow. Picture how large you would like your bank account to be at the end of the year. Count your government savings bonds. Look at them and feel them. Tell yourself how many more you want to have at the end of twelve months. If you concentrate sufficiently on these goals, you will achieve them.

Have you set your heart on spending your next vacation in France, or Bermuda, or the Canadian Rockies? See if you can't obtain travel posters picturing these places. Put them up in your den, your room, or your kitchen. Not only will they brighten up the room—they'll brighten up your subconscious and keep it working to achieve the wonderful vacation you want. Send away for travel folders too, and look at them often. The chances are that if you concentrate hard enough, and wish strongly enough, before you know it you will find yourself on an airplane or a ship, bound for the place you have been dreaming about—and pinching yourself to make sure it's really you who are going there.

Perhaps you'd like to have a fine library of books or phonograph records or a lovely wardrobe—the kind that costs hundreds and hundreds of dollars—but cannot imagine yourself being affluent enough to afford them. Your first step toward making your wish come true is not only to picture yourself rich enough, but to think concretely about the books, records, or garments you would like to have.

And don't merely think about them. Go right down to where books, phonograph records, or dresses are sold. Look at them. Consider the ones you want. When you read newspapers or magazines, pay special attention to the articles written about these things, and the advertisements.

In very short order, you will find yourself building the kind of library or wardrobe you would like to have. Your subconscious mind, stimulated by the visual impression produced by these things, will help you find ways to acquire them. So will your conscious mind. As you become more familiar with the outlets where these objects are sold, you will discover that occasionally there are sales, or that if you look carefully you can find wonderful bargains at only a fraction of the usual price. By inches or miles, faster or slower, depending upon the degree of your interest and concentration, you will achieve your ambition. Nothing can stop you!

LOSING WEIGHT

This same technique will hold for any goal you have in view. Visualize it concretely, in terms of immediate goals. If you are overweight, as so many people are, you will find this method more effective than pills in removing excess poundage. But use it as recommended. Don't merely say, "I want to lose weight"—that's too vague and abstract. Instead, picture yourself twenty pounds lighter with the attractive figure you would like to have, and the image will serve as a stirring call to forgo extra calories. Better still, get a photograph of yourself in earlier years, when you weighed less, and put it where you will see it often. Tell yourself you are going to lose two pounds a week, or whatever number is safe for your age and state of health. Get on the scales every morning and weigh yourself; the sight of your weight in bold black letters on the scale is much more effective in helping you to restrain your appetite than all the admonitions of all the physicians in the world.

A COMMON-SENSE SECRET

You see, through these simple instances, that there is nothing magical about being able to get the things you want if you visualize them as concretely and perseveringly as possible. *Dharana,* or applied concentration, is a thoroughly common-sense technique, after all.

It has been said that common sense is the one thing that everybody thinks he has enough of. Ordinary experience, however, shows us that this is not true. Some people will just lean back and dream vaguely of the things they want—the better job, the bigger bank account, the new car, the lovely home, the fine clothes, the trim figure—but they lack the common sense to take the elementary step of concentrating on immediate, concrete objectives with all their hearts and souls.

And that is the only way things are achieved in this world.

CHAPTER VI

THE SECOND SECRET

Whether you think life is worth living or not, you
will have to live it. There's no escape, no oblivion
around the corner. Time isn't destroying you, but
neither can you destroy it. Life must be lived, but of
course you can decide on what level you will live it.
That is, if you know enough and are prepared to make
the right effort. Our chief trouble now is that we
don't know enough and only make wrong efforts.
—J. B. PRIESTLEY

It was a cold morning, April 6, 1909. The sharp-
edged wind shrilled in the ears of the six men who
moved ever more slowly across the great ice sheet.
Their breath came from their nostrils in thick white
clouds. Even under their heavy furs they trembled;
fatigue made the sub-zero temperature seem even
colder.

For over a month the men had been traveling northward, ever northward, by foot and sledge over the
ice floes. Now, close to exhaustion, they stopped at a
nod from their leader. He opened an instrument case
and took measurements. Their location was 89° 57'.
His jaw set, he gazed to the north as his men squatted
on the ice.

For a few hours the travelers rested and refreshed

themselves. Even so, when their leader called to them, it seemed as though they had halted only a few moments ago, so weary were they. Slowly they lifted themselves to their feet and made ready to move on. The leader, although he walked to his sledge with difficulty, appeared to possess more strength than the others. Closeness to his goal, after so many years of hoping, lent him added energy. Across that infinite desolate expanse the tiny group of men headed into the howling wind.

Now the leader's hand went up again. The party came to a stop. The four men with slanted eyes—they were Eskimos—watched as the dark-skinned man and the white-skinned one unpacked instruments again. The white man took his measurements. A slow smile spread across his frosty face. The Eskimos felt cheered. They did not quite understand what it was all about, but the happy look on their leader's worn countenance told them more eloquently than words that an achievement of extraordinary importance had taken place.

But their leader knew. He knew it in every fiber of his being. For the first time in recorded history, human beings were standing at the North Pole.

The white man, in case you have not guessed his identity, was Commander Robert Edwin Peary of the United States Navy; the Negro was his faithful aide Henson.

It was Peary's eighth expedition to the Arctic. For twenty years he had dreamed of raising the United States flag in that barren, windy waste. To this goal he had dedicated every ounce of strength in his body—every thought in his soul—and now he had achieved his aim!

On one expedition, Peary had attempted to reach the Pole by way of northern Greenland. He went far, but then his supplies ran out. He and his men got back to the nearest Eskimo settlement barely half alive; only one of their dogs survived. Another time, his leg was crushed; on another venture he lost seven toes to frostbite. Often he lacked the money to finance his expeditions, to equip the special vessels required for polar exploration. He had to suspend his plans, and travel across the United States lecturing, making an exhausting series of one-night stands in scores of towns and cities, until little by little he accumulated the large sums of money he needed. But he won out in the end because his desire to reach the North Pole was greater than any obstacle that nature or circumstance could place in his path.

The poet Clarence Mackay has summed up the secret of this hero's superb achievement and others like it in these lines:

"If thou canst plan a noble deed,
And never flag till it succeed,
Though in the strife thy heart should bleed,
Whatever obstacles control,
Thine hour will come—go on, true soul!
Thou'lt win the prize, thou'lt reach the goal."

Peary's great deed and this poem point the way directly to the Second Secret of the Masters.

A LAW OF THE MASTERS

In the foregoing chapter, we laid great emphasis upon the need to select your goal intelligently, and offered practical suggestions for visualizing it concretely. We said that your subconscious mind is extremely responsive to concrete images, and will work to help you attain the goal you picture. Your problem, however, is to hold that goal steadfastly in mind —as steadfastly as Peary held his goal; as firmly as Edison and Andrew Carnegie held theirs . . . *If you can succeed in maintaining the picture of your desire firm and undistorted before your mind's eye, it will be projected into reality.* This is a law of the Masters.

Yes, any wish that is within the power of human beings to realize will inevitably be brought forth into tangible reality if it is concentrated upon with sufficient strength. *On the other hand, if you allow conflicting thoughts or doubts to enter your mind, they will crowd out your wish and make it impossible to achieve.*

This is not only a law of the Masters; it is a law of psychology and physiology. It is proved a thousand times a day. Here is a simple experiment you can make this instant, to see the law in action. You don't need any special equipment—test tubes, bunsen burners, chemicals, or the like. All you need is your own finger —and a thought.

TRY THIS EXPERIMENT

Hold out the index finger of your left hand. It should be fairly straight but not tense or rigid. Now tell yourself that you are going to keep it this way. At the same time, think a bit of wanting to bend your finger. Don't you notice a feeling running through your finger as though it wished to bend? The nerves are all ready to bend it—it may even start to crook slightly— but it will not bend because you decided in advance that you were only going to *think* of bending it.

Now, completely discard the idea of keeping your finger straight. Your only thought now, should be of bending it. As you hold out your finger, it immediately begins to move. The finger follows your thought obediently.

This little experiment proves, in a physical sense, the important lesson, already alluded to. *If you think of an action without a conflicting thought, your body will perform it.*

Thought, Then Action

As a matter of fact, your body may go ahead and perform a whole series of actions unconsciously once the thought of doing them has dawned in your mind; often the actions take place quite a while after the initial thought. Much of your ordinary behavior occurs on this subconscious basis.

Let's consider, for example, the everyday matter of dressing yourself. After you get out of bed in the morning, the first thought that crosses your mind concerns the putting on of your clothing. You may still be half asleep or lost in a reverie, but a few moments later you will observe that you are partly or entirely dressed. You may not recall the various steps of dressing—putting on your shoes, socks, and underwear—but you have gone through them. If there is no opposition to the thought, it will fulfill itself. Psychologists describe this as ideo-motor action. First there is an idea—and then the motor mechanism of your body, guided by your subconscious mind, carries it out in intricate detail without any further thought on your part.

Every twenty-four hours you perform thousands of

ideo-motor actions. Suppose, as a second example, that you are visiting a friend and talking to him. On the end table, near you, there are dishes of chocolates and nuts. The idea fleets through your mind that they look very tasty. As you talk, you find that from time to time your hand is going to these dishes and carrying some candy or nuts to your mouth. The action in no way interrupts your train of thought as you converse with your friend, and you are hardly, if at all, conscious of it. The thought, once it occurs to you, will be fulfilled if there is no obstacle to its fulfillment.

This interesting phenomenon has been well described by the German scientist Lotze in his epochal work, *Medical Psychology:*

"We see in writing or playing the piano a large number of exceedingly complicated movements following quickly one upon the other, the original ideas for which remained barely an instant in consciousness, certainly not long enough to awaken any other thought than the general one of resigning oneself without reserve to the passing over of idea into action. All the acts of our daily life happen in this way: Our standing up, walking, talking, all this never demands a distinct impulse of the will, but is adequately brought about by the pure flux of thought."

WHY IDEAS COME TO NOTHING

On the other hand, as you very well know, there are many cases when the ideas in your mind come to nothing. Take, for example, the problem you face sometimes in getting out of your warm bed on a cold morning. You have the thought of getting up but you may not act upon it for minutes or hours, much though you

93

feel you should. Why not, if thought is so compelling?

The answer lies in the fact that your thoughts are contradictory: you wish to get up, but you also want to enjoy the comfort of staying in your bed. As Professor William James has put it:

"Every representation of a movement awakens in some degree the actual movement which is its object; and awakens it in a maximum degree whenever it is not kept from so doing by an antagonistic representation present simultaneously to the mind."

It is this fact which explains why so many of our fine resolutions come to nothing. We have our goals in mind, but we have thoughts that keep us from achieving them. We want to get ahead in the world—but the poverty thought, the failure thought, the sickness thought weaken or contradict our success thoughts. They prevent our truly positive thoughts from working themselves out.

You Must Be One-Pointed

In all the writings and teachings of the Masters, there is a term that recurs again and again, like the refrain of a song. It is the word "one-pointed." One-pointedness is the heart of *dharana,* or concentration —the core of any practical method for success. The man who is truly one-pointed, according to the Masters, is destiny's darling.

What is one-pointedness? Says the *guru* Patanjali:

"When you have learned to control your mind in the face of disturbances, then your mind has acquired one-pointedness. This quality is a state or condition of the mind."

One-pointedness is the ability to exclude from your

94

mind all thoughts but the one you want it to be possessed by. It is the power to concentrate on your dream until it has become more than a dream. It is a suit of self-forged armor, hard and shining, that deflects all distractions and hardships while you move unerringly toward the fulfillment of your wishes.

THE HIGHEST IS WITHIN YOUR REACH

Perhaps one-pointedness sounds difficult to acquire. Its acquisition is, in a sense, the hardest part of the method of the Masters. Still, they have achieved it, and so, too, have many others. What one man or woman has done, others can do. You are of their blood. The highest is within your reach, if you wish it strongly enough.

With practice, one-pointedness can be achieved by anyone, Patanjali tells us. There are many techniques of building it within yourself; some have already been explained and still more will be revealed to you as we proceed. If you persevere in them, one-pointedness should soon become a habit with you. Before long the fruits of fortune will tumble into your lap.

"Sustained one-pointedness," says Patanjali, "leads to samadhi"—that is, bliss. One-pointedness brings extraordinary powers within your grasp. It mobilizes the subconscious mind, giving you incredible strength and effectiveness. Like a bright sun, it shoots rays of might into your deeper being, warming it and bringing to life positive qualities for success that most human beings do not even know they possess.

Because it brings your subconscious powers into play, one-pointedness grows easier with practice. Although it may be attained only spasmodically at first, in time it becomes second nature. After a while you will find your subconscious mind working for you almost without bidding, smoothing your way to achievement. Things that seemed difficult to accomplish will become easy. Your friends will wonder at your fearlessness, your confidence in the face of difficulties, your ability to perform hard work with miraculous ease and speed. Above all, they will marvel at your will power.

FUNCTIONING AS A WHOLE PERSON

The one-pointed person gets what he wants because he functions as a *whole person*—on a physical, mental, and subconscious level. The subconscious mind gives multiple effectiveness to the conscious mind and the body, causing all three to work in harmony.

The blocks that exist in the minds of most people, keeping them from utilizing their capacities to the fullest, are eliminated in the one-pointed person. Fearful thoughts, lack of self-confidence, fatigue, and other factors that paralyze us when success is within our grasp are wiped away; self-mastery is complete.

NEGATIVE AND POSITIVE THINKING

The first thing you must realize, if you want to attain one-pointedness, is the danger of contrary thoughts. Earlier we dwelt upon the baneful power that negative thoughts have to weaken and harm you. The opposite is equally true: *Thoughts of success, achievement, and health will help you to health, achievement, and success.*

As we observed in the teachings of the Masters, thoughts have reality; they differ from physical objects in form but not in their essential nature as manifestations of electrical energy. Traveling through your body and your mind as electrical energy, they make these function to your benefit or disadvantage in proportion as they are positive or negative.

To be 100 per cent one-pointed, you must make your thoughts 100 per cent positive. The more you allow negative thoughts, either through indifference or lack of self-faith, to dominate your mind, the less will you be able to do or get what you want. As the Masters put it, you run the risk of becoming "many-pointed," and of discharging your energy to no good purpose.

Obstacles in Your Path

What are the obstacles that arise to diffuse your one-pointedness? Patanjali catalogued them centuries ago, and they are still the same today. He lists them in this order: "Ill health, boredom, self-doubt, carelessness, laziness, worldly-mindedness, incapacity to perceive what is needed, a tendency to be misled into side issues after a certain measure of success has been achieved, and incapacity to adhere to your purpose." In the complex world of the West, there are even more harmful forces than those the Hindu Patanjali mentions.

Some of these obstacles we shall deal with in due course, but the main ones we shall examine at this point. Patanjali gives a number of methods for overcoming them, but the one that is most important for the man and woman of the Western world is psychological. For Patanjali says: "Those obstacles may be prevented by steady and intense concentration on some

97

subject." Next he offers us specific advice; he says: "If you wish to eliminate harmful thoughts, attitudes, and feelings, you should concentrate upon their opposites. It is wise to eliminate them; such thoughts hamper progress in yoga and will cause you to be unhappy."

CONTRARY CONCENTRATION

Every condition or quality that exists in the world has an opposite. In fact, it is because they have opposites that it is possible for us to know them. If there were no night, there would be no day as such. If no one were lazy, a man could not call himself industrious. If disease did not exist, we would have no idea of health. All conditions are paired with their opposites, but of each pair only one condition will benefit us. The other brings harm and failure, if we permit it to possess our minds.

The meditation on opposites counseled by Patanjali is, in these pages, termed Contrary Concentration, or Concentration on the Positive. It offers a method not only of wiping failure-producing thoughts from the mind and attaining one-pointedness, but of improving your character and making yourself a better, more effective human being.

The method, superficially, seems simple. After all, what could be easier than to think of cheerfulness when you feel depressed, to dwell upon the value of confidence when you begin to doubt yourself? The difficulty, however, is this: your negative thoughts have easily as much vitality as your positive ones, sometimes more. Only after prolonged meditation, on many different occasions, can you perfect yourself in the technique of Contrary Concentration.

In your Contrary Concentration, as in ordinary concentration, you must immerse yourself in your thought, until it fills your entire being. You must meditate upon it from every conceivable angle great or small. Only then will the thoughts or qualities you wish to possess become capable of implanting themselves solidly in your subconscious mind, from which they will thereafter flow forth automatically. Only then will you be able to uproot the harmful thoughts and make your subconscious mind so firm that self-damaging notions will not be able to take root in it, no matter how often they cast their seed upon it.

CONCENTRATION OF THE MASTERS

Concentration, as practiced by the Masters of the Far East, is far different from what the term ordinarily means to us of the West. The saintly seer of India, Ramakrisha, has out of personal experience painted a telling picture of what Oriental meditation is like. He has said:

"In the grove I would sit, in deep meditation, with my body perfectly still, and lose all consciousness of the outside world. Birds would perch on my head. Often snakes would crawl over my motionless body. The ordinary man would not be able to bear a fraction of the tremendous fervour I felt."

When, in accordance with Hindu ritual, Ramakrishna uttered the mystical syllable *Rang* and imagined himself surrounded by a wall of flame, he actually felt the heat of the mythical fire blistering his skin. His was one-pointedness in the highest sense.

How to Begin

For your own Contrary Concentration, the best procedure is this:

Select a quiet place where you will not be disturbed; it might be your den, study, or bedroom. Seat yourself in a comfortable position and remove your shoes, tie, and any garments that constrict your body. When you feel completely relaxed and at ease, but not before, begin your meditation.

If you are a religious person, commune for a few moments with God. Pray to Him for help, in the manner that suits you best. Any prayer will do, so long as it renews your feeling of kinship to the Almighty. As you pray, reach out and feel His friendliness for you. Open your heart to His Love. Recognize that He created you in His Own Image, and that He wants only happiness and joy for you.

The Masters of the Far East, when they commence meditation, do much the same thing. They pray, too, though they call their divinity by such names as Siva or Buddha. They bring themselves, just as you do, into harmony with the Central Power of the Universe and drink in His Power and His Strength.

The Second Stage

When you feel yourself in tune with the Infinite, you are ready to enter upon the second stage of your meditation. For the subject of your Contrary Concentration, select some quality that you know is essential to the fruition of your plans, but in which you are deficient. It might be Interest, Diligence, Confidence, Calmness, Persistence, Desire for Success; all these and more intertwine in any substantial achievement, and are fit subjects for Contrary Concentration. However, since in this chapter we are fundamentally concerned with one-pointedness, the sample topic selected for contrary meditation will be an item in Patanjali's list of human qualities that weaken concentration. He calls this quality the "tendency to be misled into side issues." Other names will do as well. You can call it "losing sight of one's objective," "many-pointedness," or a "tendency to succumb to distractions," if you prefer.

Your goal—the subject you tend to wander away from—is already known to you. It is the thing closest to your heart—promotion in your job, wealth, artistic achievement, good health, social success, or whatever other objective you have selected. Let us suppose that you pursue this aim when you think of it, but not consistently enough, since you are not yet one-pointed. Success means work, and work is often unpleasant to us. As the days go by, you frequently find yourself doing things that do not help you at all to reach your objective. One night you feel you'd rather watch a ball game on television; another night you spend listening to music; or you agree to give a few evenings to doing publicity for your club—a worthy project, but one that hardly contributes to your success. This behavior is the manifestation of the negative tendency Patanjali mentions.

WHY HE AND NOT YOU?

Your Contrary Concentration, aimed at combatting this tendency, may last only a few moments, or hours may be devoted to it—but it should be repeated often if you want it to be helpful. To start with, you might picture to yourself the achievement of someone you are personally acquainted with.

Almost every one of us knows some person who was once close to us but has gone much further in life. It may be someone you used to play with as a child, who sat in the same classroom with you at school, or who worked in the same office with you. Possibly you have not seen him recently, but every once in a while you may read about him in the newspapers, or some mutual acquaintance may give you a report about what he has been doing. Perhaps you have learned that he has just bought a thirty-thousand-dollar house, that his business is expanding by leaps and bounds, or that he has written a best-selling novel. Being human, you are irked by his success, when you compare it to your own. Indeed, you may recall very concretely that when you knew this individual, you found him singularly unimpressive. Perhaps you received better marks at school than he did and were more intelligent and capable in general than he.

Why does he make the grade while you hardly seem to get ahead at all? Ask yourself that question, as part of your meditation.

Comparisons, it has well been said, are invidious, so make them honestly, in order to find the answer. Of course you may be worthier than your rival, and have greater latent possibilities for success. In one respect, however, you may be sure you are surpassed by him: in one-pointedness. From the start, he has never lost sight of his goal. Because his energy is not dissipated in idleness or side issues, everything he does is aimed at the ultimate achievement. You, however, persistently allow yourself to be distracted.

Of course you may be able to adduce plausible reasons for your lesser degree of achievement, but the fact remains that you have not gotten as far as he has, have you?

Don't Rationalize

In comparing yourself to this more successful contemporary, do not make the error of seeking consolation in the notion that he is more self-centered.

You may momentarily salve your sense of self-esteem by telling yourself that you are less egotistical and mean—that you do not want to get ahead by walking upon the backs of others. It may make you feel fine to say that he exploited connections and friendships, and that you could never be so self-seeking. But, in the final analysis, aren't you saying that he had a stronger drive, a deeper desire to achieve than you?

Everyone who gets ahead is not necessarily selfish or mean. Earlier we saw that a great doer like Andrew Carnegie gave much of what he earned for philanthropic purposes. So, too, did Rockefeller and Ford. Men like Admiral Peary and Stonewall Jackson never exploited anyone.

It is mere rationalization to attribute our failures to superiority of character. We may indeed be superior in many ways—but not in that absolute devotion to a goal that the Masters call one-pointedness and the unsuccessful call pigheadedness.

The Masters of the East, with their profound insight into the human heart, were able to see clearly that our failures, by and large, are rooted in our weaknesses. From their own experience in the arduous study of yoga, they knew how easily people were distracted from their purpose. Think long and hard upon these words of Patanjali: "Some who would succeed are but dabblers, some are earnest in their efforts, but only a handful are completely one-pointed." Do you want to drift with the multitude, or move purposefully toward success with the few?

No Prize Without Effort

Having analyzed the fundamental reason for the achievement of your acquaintance, it is now time to turn your thoughts to others whose accomplishments are even greater.

Travel back in time. You live in the most wonderful land on earth, where men, for the first time in history, are truly free, and enjoy access to the comforts and conveniences of an advanced civilization. It was not always so. Visualize, for a while, the tremendous risks that were run by America's pioneers.

Mile by mile, those determined men had to fight their way across a dangerous, hostile continent. They had to level forests and make the land fertile; the labors they performed were almost never-ending, but the rewards they reaped were in proportion. Realize clearly that there is no prize without some sacrifice.

Learn of Noble Men

You may go further back in time, and meditate upon individual great men whose lives offer models of one-pointedness. Shakespeare once said: "For mine own part, I shall be glad to learn of noble men." You can draw great inspiration from them, to strengthen your Contrary Concentration.

The One-pointedness of Columbus

No hardship, criticism, or adversity could daunt the one-pointedness of Christopher Columbus; nothing could distract him from his conviction that he could discover a new route to the Indies by sailing westward. Yet hardships and criticisms he encountered aplenty. One after another the crowned heads of Europe turned away from his great project in disdain. First it was John, King of Portugal. Then it was the rulers of Spain, Ferdinand and Isabella, who were too deeply involved in a war with the Moors to lend of their treasure to the visionary Italian sea captain.

Picture how heartbroken an ordinary man might be at these rebuffs, but how persistent Columbus was in the face of them. He was already en route to visit the King of France when he was summoned back to the Spanish Court. At last, after ten years of attempting to persuade the Spanish potentates to extend the necessary financial support, his plans looked as though they might bear fruit.

But not yet. Columbus, like you, dreamed high, and he desired high rewards. He wanted a share of the minerals that would be discovered in the lands beyond the seas, and he wanted the title of "Admiral of the Ocean Sea." The Spaniards turned him down again.

Columbus packed his bags, ready to set out again for France. But one of the royal counselors was convinced that Columbus could succeed in reaching the Indies, and was ready to finance his voyage. He brought Columbus back, and this time it was agreed that he would sail.

Think of the old French saying that the first step is the hardest. For Columbus, the first step was hard and every step thereafter was harder still. Compared to his lot, yours is easy. When he had his ships, he could not find a crew. Spain's sailors were fearful of unknown waters. Men that were rotting in foul dungeons, although offered their freedom and good pay if they would go along with him, preferred their chains to the terrors of the ocean to the west. After much trying, Columbus finally was able to muster enough of a crew to man his three vessels. On August 3, 1492, the little fleet set sail.

Three days out of port a mishap befell the intrepid voyager. A rudder broke loose from one of his ships. But that did not make Columbus despair of success. With his mind's eye he saw new lands over the horizon; he would not let an accident keep him from them. After the rudder had been repaired, there was more trouble. The needle of the ship's compass began to move erratically. The men were disturbed and wanted to turn back. But Columbus was equal to any challenge, and he managed to allay their fears and convince them that all was well.

About six weeks out of Spain, the sailors saw a strange sight. Not far ahead of their vessels a meteor fell from the skies and plunged hissing into the sea. To the superstitious folk of that day a meteor was an omen of approaching disaster. The sailors believed that they must be close to the edge of the earth, and the meteor was a sign that they should turn back. Columbus felt they were wrong, but he could not be sure; no ships in known history had ever sailed so far westward, and the unknown holds peril for almost all of us. But Columbus' desire to see what lay beyond was greater than his fear, and the tiny fleet traveled on.

Less than a week later, some birds were sighted. To the mariners of that day, this was sure proof that land was near. They took heart, and peered constantly into the horizon for the first glimpse of shore.

But there were still weeks of sailing ahead of them. It was not until October 12 that Columbus, peering into the night, saw a light far off. Early the next morning the ships actually reached land. The voyage had taken many, many days—but a whole new world had been discovered, bringing about an incredible change in the fortunes of Spain, which became the richest land on earth, and doubling the size of the known world. In honor of the great accomplishment of Columbus, to this very day his lineal descendant in Spain bears the title of Admiral of the Ocean Sea. And all of this only because the one-pointedness of one man was so perfect that it did not permit him to be distracted from his purpose!

ASSOCIATING NEGATIVE AND POSITIVE

In this wise should you meditate upon the lives of great men and their accomplishments. You should search your soul and discover the true reasons why you lose your one-pointedness and are misled into side issues. Counter each distraction or worry with affirmative thoughts about the value of effort and devotion to work, and the substantial rewards these can bring. To every negative thought, tie a positive one, so that they are indissolubly associated in your mind on both levels, conscious and subconscious.

To the negative thought: "I'm too tired to work," tie the positive thought: *"Once I start working and become absorbed in my labors, my fatigue will fall away, and I will be able to do much."*

To the negative thought: "I have a headache," tie the positive thought: *"Headaches are often born of boredom or mental conflict. Work will drive it away."*

To the negative thought: "I don't have the time to work," tie the positive thought: *"The busiest people accomplish the most. With intelligent planning I can find time for all that is essential."*

To the negative thought: "I can't," tie the positive thought: *"I can if I want to strongly enough."*

To the negative thought: "I feel too ill to work," apply the positive thought: *"My mind is as healthy as I want it to be. Much illness is imagined; pain is great if I think it is great, little if I think it is little. Sick men, blind men, crippled men have accomplished more than unhandicapped persons who lacked one-pointedness."*

The more closely you link these positive thoughts to the negative ones, the easier it will be to shake off damaging notions and do the things you want to do. After a while, substituting the positive for the negative will become habitual, like braking your car when you see a red light at the street corner. Whenever you find a negative thought in your mind, it should be a signal for you to replace it with a positive one.

Practice Contrary Concentration often. It will make you strong against all opposition, whether it be without or within. It will protect you against all the misfortunes of life. It was John Milton, the man who won world-wide fame in literature although he was completely blind, who said: "The mind is its own place, and in itself can make a heaven of hell, a hell of heaven."

CHAPTER VII

THE THIRD SECRET

Our minds are finite, and yet even in these circumstances of finitude we are surrounded by possibilities
that are infinite, and the purpose of human life is to
grasp as much as we can of that infinitude.
                              —ALFRED NORTH WHITEHEAD

"When things go wrong, as they sometimes will,
  When the road you're trudging seems all up hill,
  When the funds are low and the debts are high,
  And you want to smile, but you have to sigh,
  When care is pressing you down a bit,
  Rest, if you must—but don't you quit.

"Life is queer with its twists and turns,
  As every one of us sometimes learns,
  And many a failure turns about
  When he might have won had he stuck it out;
  Don't give up, though the pace seems slow—
  You might succeed with another blow.

"Often the goal is nearer than
  It seems to a faint and faltering man,
  Often the struggler has given up
  When he might have captured the victor's cup.
  And he learned too late, when the night slipped down,
  How close he was to the golden crown.

"Success is failure turned inside out—
   The silver tint of the clouds of doubt—
   And you never can tell how close you are,
   It may be near when it seems afar;
   So stick to the fight when you're hardest hit—
   It's when things seem worst that you mustn't quit."

MISTAKING APPEARANCE FOR REALITY

All of us, on occasion, mistake the appearance for the reality. If a man smiles at us, we suppose he likes us. If an acquaintance walks by us frowning, we imagine that his feelings towards us are unfriendly. But the first man may just be pretending, and the second man's grim aspect may be caused by some personal misfortune.

As we mistake others, so we mistake ourselves. Some of us have immense but untried capacities for achievement. We are potential Lincolns, Edisons, Shakespeares, or Henry Fords. But we lack the faith required to prove our abilities, and we belittle our every word and deed. Underrating our own powers, because we see ourselves as drab, incompetent mediocrities, we are afraid to embark upon the very enterprises that will reveal to the world and ourselves the potent persons that in our hearts we feel ourselves to be.

Perhaps, years ago, some short-sighted older brother or sister, father or teacher told us we would never amount to much. Swayed by the authority of the speaker, we mistook those heartless words for the truth. It may be, too, that we were frustrated in a few small endeavors, and supposed that henceforth failure had to be our destiny. In one way or another, the things that people said or the misfortunes that we suffered gave us a demeaning, embittering picture of ourselves and our abilities. In a sensitive period we took this image to ourselves and modeled ourselves upon it. We lost all awareness of the forceful, able persons we really were. We were taken in by false appearances.

Are You Aware of Your Powers?

"Through concentration," declares an ancient sage of the Far East, "a man becomes aware of himself. By and large, the individual loses himself in his own distorted picture of life because he identifies himself with it."

Note the emphasis placed by the sage upon awareness; he is telling us that the man who is aware of himself has found himself; the man who lacks awareness is virtually a lost soul.

Can you honestly say that you have a genuine awareness of yourself and your powers? Do you see yourself as the vital, gifted person you were meant to be? Or, duped by a distorted picture of life, do you regard yourself as a born second-rater, a failure, a man or woman without a future?

If you belong to this second category, an enormous boulder blocks your route to success. Your way will be difficult, if not impassable, until the obstacle has been removed.

Before you can hope to remove it, you must be prepared to face the truth about yourself. You must be willing to look at your picture of life and admit that it is a false one.

This is not nearly so easy as it sounds. Most people keep running away from the truth as though it were something hateful. The words once engraved upon the temple of the oracle at Delphi—"Know thyself"— are among the hardest in the world to take to heart.

Your Enemies—False Ideas

Your picture of life, or, basically speaking, the thoughts you have in mind, can be your worst enemies if they are distorted and confused. Until you know them for what they are, you cannot fight them. Once you recognize their true nature, however, you will be well on the way to routing the damaging thoughts and replacing them with others that are constructive and charged with power.

Now is the time to try a little self-diagnosis. Just as the doctor gives you a checkup to determine the state of your health, here is a series of questions that will help you to ascertain whether your mental picture of yourself and the world is accurate and helpful, or confused and damaging. Think carefully as you answer the following ten questions:

Answer Yes or No

1. Do you believe, with regard to people, that "you can't teach an old dog new tricks"?

2. Do you often feel bored or listless?

3. In your opinion, will the future be an unvaried repetition of the present—and pretty dreary at that?

4. Do you often hesitate to undertake new projects out of fear that you will not be equal to them?

5. Does it depress you to mingle with people who are better dressed or who have more money than you?

6. Do you have a pervasive feeling that the breaks in life are against you?

7. Are your fundamental convictions—about poli-

tics, human behavior, morality, and progress—pretty much what they were ten or twenty years ago?

8. Do you frequently find yourself envying others?

9. Do you have an inferiority complex?

10. Do you generally stammer or feel timid when you are with your boss or people whose station in life is higher than yours?

If, to seven or more of these questions, your answer is yes, then it is safe to say that you have a confused awareness of yourself—and as a result you are prevented from performing many of the great things you are capable of. Fortunately, if you have an open mind, you can remedy this handicap. On the other hand, if you have answered no to all or most of the questions, your case is much better. Still, nobody's situation is so good that it cannot be improved.

AT THE MERCY OF DISTORTIONS

The truth is that all of us, except those who have learned the merits of one-pointedness, are at the mercy of the distortions that imperfect understanding creates in our minds. Unless we are constantly on our guard, we easily fall victim to what the Masters of the Far East call *maya,* or illusion. We plunge into the false picture we have formed of the world and wander about in it lost and bewildered, like men and women in a hall of mirrors.

Have you ever walked into a great, luxurious place —say the lobby of the Waldorf or some other exclusive hotel—and been overcome by a feeling of insignificance? You see tremendous walls rising to an ornate ceiling scores of feet overhead, you walk on thick carpets and are jostled by hurrying, well-dressed people. Unless you are on your guard, a sense of the vastness of the building and the superiority of the people who ordinarily frequent it almost overcomes you, and you feel very humble and insecure.

In this situation, you have formed a distorted picture. It dwarfs you, and your identity is lost in it.

Have you ever gone into your employer's office to ask for a favor or a raise? Your superior may sit at a large mahogany desk, so much handsomer than yours; on it you may see an expensive desk set and a silver cigarette lighter. Before him there is a stack of bills and correspondence, and, as he looks up at you from them, you wonder whether you have the right to disturb him. On the walls, frowning down at you, are the photographs of former presidents of the organization; their nearness gives you a profound sense of smallness.

The picture made by all these things on your mind is a distorted one again. It is not reality, but an appearance, in which you lose yourself.

TRUE PICTURES

The true picture is a far different one. You cannot even see it unless you have the self-awareness the Oriental sage speaks of. That self-awareness, he says, you can attain by concentration. It is Contrary Concentration which combats the illusions forced upon you by unfamiliar persons and circumstances.

And what will be the focal point of your Contrary Concentration? First, the thought that you were created in the image of God. Your life goes back through countless generations to the root of all life. You are a son or a daughter of God, King of the Universe. Royal houses and principalities may come and go, but the house of God, your Father, will stand forever. He gives His Love freely to all His children, if they will but take it. Wrapped in His kingly mantle, why should you feel inferior to anyone?

Second, in a naturalistic sense, realize that you, as a human being, are the peak of creation. Scientists estimate that the earth is over two billion years old. There are some one million different kinds of creatures alive today, ranging from microscopic animals to the great apes; millions more lived in ages past, but of these only vestiges remain. Are you fully aware that you are a member of the most intelligent and capable species that ever walked the face of the earth: *Homo sapiens,* or "Wise man"? Life has been in a process of development for untold aeons, and the most creative, most perfect creature ever begotten is—*you!*

By God's word and by the verdict of science, truly you are Lord of the World.

In your concentration, take another look around the lobby of the Waldorf, or any other place that inspires you with awe. What are the walls but plaster, stone, wood, and metal, which men like you put together? What are the luxurious tapestries and rugs but simple vegetable or animal matter, given shape, texture, and color by men like you? You have life, and walls and rugs do not—why should they intimidate you?

The richly attired, affluent persons who walk about in such places—what are they but people like yourself? They may happen to have more money and prestige than you have yet achieved, but they are not made of better flesh, bone, or blood than you; they have the same bodily functions as you, the same desires and weaknesses. If they do not watch their health, they probably won't live as long as you will.

In their mortality, as in the sight of God and the law, they are at best your equals.

These are the thoughts you should have in mind

when you enter your employer's office, or call on some person whose patronage means much to you. What is the lavishly furnished office but a structure of inert materials? As a living creature you are far superior to them. And the man himself, whose favor you seek? He's an important personage, no doubt, but how important would he be without you and people like you? He would be spending his entire life wresting his food and clothing from Nature, and enjoying a bare subsistence at best. Is he immortal, or made of finer stuff than you? No, you're both human beings, cut from the same cloth. If your efforts make his lot in life easier, he knows you are very valuable to him, and he will give your request earnest consideration.

The Practice of Awareness

Practice an awareness of your powers. Do not allow the appearance of things and people to submerge your individuality. A room is only a room, though it be an imposing one in a palace, or the main office of a giant corporation; a man is only a man, though for a brief while he bears the title of King, President, or Chairman of the Board. And you? You are his equal. You are the Word Made Flesh. You are bursting with powers, and all you need is confidence to bring them forth.

Realize that you are mighty, and in short order you will actually be mighty. Put fear out of your mind, and you will be filled with self-trust. You can and must learn to stand on your own feet, to march forward, and do the work that your soul tells you to do. If you trust in your ability, you will discover new abilities within yourself. Strong in faith, like Moses, you can ask the sea to divide, the rock to give forth water, and they will obey your command.

Trust Thyself

Ralph Waldo Emerson, the sage of Concord, who drank deeply of the wisdom of the Masters of the Far East, once said: "God will not have his work made manifest by cowards. . . . Trust thyself: every heart vibrates to that iron string." And in your own Bible you will read: "The kingdom of God is within you." It is the will of God that you should be fearless, and have more of the good things of the world. "I have come," said Jesus, "that they might have life, and that they might have it more abundantly." It does not please God that you, His child, should eke out a pitiful existence in self-doubt and poverty.

"Trust in thine own untried capacity
As thou wouldst trust in God Himself. Thy soul
Is but an emanation from the whole.

"Thou dost not dream what forces lie in thee.
Vast and unfathomed as the grandest sea.
Thy silent mind o'er diamond caves may roll;
Go seek them, but let Pilot Will control
Those passions which thy favoring winds can be.

"No man shall place a limit to thy strength;
Such triumphs as no mortal ever gained
May yet be thine if thou wilt but believe
In thy Creator and in thyself. At length
Some feet will tread all heights now unattained—
Why not thine own? Press on! achieve! achieve!"

The Inmost Becomes the Outmost

When you are assailed by doubt or uncertainty, that is the time to remember the Law of the Masters: *Always the inmost becomes the outmost.*

Life is potentiality. It is a screen, high and wide, and perfectly blank, ever ready to reflect the images your thoughts cast upon it. If you picture yourself as a small and impotent person, a plaything of circumstance, that is what you will be. If you have consciousness of your powers and view yourself as the equal of all, a maker and creator, that is what life will show you to be.

As You Think, So You Will Be

The world never stands still. It is a constant becoming. The face of the earth—as well as the face you see in the mirror—offers clear evidence that all is flux and change.

Each year the earth renews itself and is different. Each year your body renews itself; you are not this year exactly the same person you were a year ago. Dr. Paul C. Aebersold, director of the isotopes division of the Atomic Energy Commission, says that "Tracer studies show that the atomic turnover in our bodies is quite rapid. . . . in a year approximately 98 per cent of the atoms in us now will be replaced by other atoms that we take in our air, food, and drink."

Minds do not change so often as bodies. They hardly change at all, unless we sincerely want them to. Are you an old dog that can't learn "new tricks"? If that is what you think, so you will be. If, however, you draw yourself out of your distorted picture of the world; if you imbue yourself with a sense of creativity and eagerness to understand and accomplish—you can learn such new tricks as will astound the world.

Need the future be an unvaried repetition of the present? No, it cannot be, it will not be. To the casual eye, history seems to move in cycles, and the present is the faithful echo of the past. Were that true, you, being your father's son, would be your father all over again; you could be no more than he. But the truth is that you are different in face and in capacity. Think yourself like him and you will be like him; think yourself better, work to make yourself better, and no perversity of chance can stop you from being better. This is as true of nations as it is of individuals. America in the twentieth century is not America in the nineteenth. It is a far brighter, richer land, and only because men wanted it to be so.

LIGHT YOUR CANDLE

Do you envy others because they possess more of the world's goods than you? Then you are guilty of a distortion—you have projected the poverty thought upon the screen of life. "It is better," say the Masters, "to light a candle than to curse the darkness." If you took the energy you dissipate in envy and applied it to constructive thinking about how to better your situation, sooner or later you would outstrip those whose circumstances fire you with envy.

THE SECRET OF BEAUTY

Are you dismayed in the company of others because you think yourself ugly? None of God's creatures are ugly unless they believe themselves to be so. A serene, confident mind emanates such charm and beauty, that the physical appearance is transfigured. If you think beautiful, friendly thoughts and utter them aloud to others, people will find you more attractive than any hero or heroine of the theater. But if your mind, confused and distorted, dwells on thoughts of ugliness and inferiority, the world will see you as ugly and inferior.

We love people because they have loving thoughts of us, not because they are beautiful.

Open your mind, open your soul. Let all good, kind, constructive things in; drive out all notions of fear, inferiority, weakness, hate, illness, and ugliness. These last are distortions, and they will twist you and warp you.

Negative thoughts kill, but positive thoughts give life, power, and happiness, now and hereafter.

CHAPTER VIII

THE FOURTH SECRET

I begin to understand that the promises of the world
are for the most part vain phantoms, and that to have
faith in oneself and become something of worth and
value is the best and safest course.

—MICHELANGELO

Millions of people all over the globe revere the name
of Martin Luther. In the history of world religions,
it is one of the great names. It is almost synonymous
with the word Protestant.

The man, Martin Luther, however, was hardly a
prepossessing figure, or a brilliant one. A man of the
people, of peasant origin, he occasionally used poor
language; when he was with his betters, he appeared
diffident and ill at ease. Much of his writing is drab
and dull.

When Europe first heard of Luther, he was an
Augustinian brother, a professor at the University of
Wittenberg, a little-known college in Germany. He
came to greatness almost by accident. Although his
preaching caused the venerable structure of the Catholic Church to split asunder, that was far from his intention in the beginning; he merely wanted to call the

attention of the faithful to certain abuses prevalent among the clergy.

In the pitiless floodlight of history, Luther the man appears as a mediocrity.

Still, there were many other religious reformers in that age—brilliant men like Wycliffe, Erasmus, Huss. Why did Luther succeed in changing the faith of multitudes while these others achieved less spectacular success?

Luther began to gain a wide reputation in his middle thirties, when he nailed his famous theses to the door of the church of the castle of Wittenberg. In these theses, Luther attacked the sale of indulgences by the Catholic Church. Indulgences were documents giving official forgiveness for sins. Luther condemned their sale because he held that if a man believes he will find salvation, it will surely come to him through God's mercy. Faith, not money, buys salvation, he maintained.

In those days, to propound such ideas was the same as signing your own death warrant. Luther was charged with heresy, one of the grimmest accusations that could be made in that age of intense religious fervour. He was summoned by the emperor, Charles the Fifth, to appear before the Diet of the city of Worms.

Luther's friends told him not to go. They were certain that he would be found guilty and executed. "Run away," they told him.

But Martin Luther did not know the meaning of fear, for he was convinced that his views were correct, and that they must triumph. "No," said he, "I will go there, even though I should encounter three times as many demons as there are tiles on the house tops."

Warned that a certain Duke George in particular was bent upon his downfall, Luther replied: "I will go there though for nine whole days running it should rain Duke Georges."

BUOYED UP BY SELF-FAITH

Buoyed up by self-faith, Luther set out upon his fateful journey to Worms. Coming in sight of the ancient bell tower of the city, he stood up in his wagon and sang *"Ein feste Burg ist unser Gott"*—*"A mighty fortress is our Lord"*—a song which he had just composed, and which was destined to become the battle cry of the Reformation.

In the Diet, Emperor Charles urged Luther to retract his heretical opinions. Luther did not quail before the monarch's wrath, but sustained his point of view. His words give us the measure of the man. "I can and will retract nothing," he said, "as it is dangerous and dishonorable to act against one's conscience." In a strong voice he declared, "Here I stand. I cannot do otherwise. God help me!"

The Diet outlawed Luther. He was named a heretic, subject to the penalty of death. Fortunately he had a guarantee of safety until his return home. On the journey back to Wittenberg he disappeared, and many supposed he had been murdered by those who condemned his opinions. In reality, however, he was spirited away by an admirer, Frederick the Wise, Elector of Saxony, who had Luther taken to his castle in Thuringia, where he would be safe from his foes.

The confidence and the ably stated convictions of Martin Luther attracted still other powerful defenders to his side. It was not long before he was the founder of a church with millions of adherents. Such is the power of faith in oneself and one's beliefs over the minds of mankind. It is in this immense self-trust that we find the secret of Luther's success.

Why You Must Believe in Yourself

The men who amount to anything in this world—as religious leaders, warriors, inventors, industrialists, sales executives, artists, writers, musicians, scientists —are not always geniuses. Those who know them well do not hesitate to label many of them mediocrities. But, though they may lack brilliance, there is one compensating feature they have in common—all possess a colossal faith in their convictions and in their ability to succeed. They never doubt themselves, but embark on each new venture convinced that its outcome will be precisely what they desire.

If, like these men, you believe with your entire heart and soul in what you are doing, tremendous forces are released in your subconscious mind. No effort seems too great when you have confidence in yourself. Faith fills you with inspiration. Concentration becomes easier. You dwell in a state akin to ecstasy—and the Masters of the Far East have said that all things obey a soul elevated into ecstasy.

If you question your abilities or the worthiness of your enterprises, the latter will hardly seem worth the pains they cost, and you will find that you give only a part of yourself to them. Obstacles will be magnified in your imagination; your powers will not be equal to the demands placed upon them. So take the opposite tack. Obey this imperative rule for success: *Conduct*

yourself as though it were impossible for you to fall
short of your goal.

How to Exorcize Doubts

Before you start anything, exorcize your doubts as Jesus exorcized devils. Picture yourself as a doer and achiever, projecting your will upon the blank screen of life. Concentrate on the success thought. Tell yourself that you are completely capable of performing what lies before you, and of much, much more.

The Masters have ever held that a confident attitude is the most important equipment you can have for any undertaking. Brilliant ideas, tremendous knowledge, and large sums of money are unavailing and great enterprises come to naught where confidence fails.

If You Have Faith

It is surprising but true that if you have faith in yourself, others will have faith in you. In any arena of endeavor, the person with definite convictions carries weight. You would never buy from a salesman who did not convince you that his product was superior. You would not listen for long to a lecturer who did not sound as though he himself believed what he was saying. If a doctor did not seem to think he could cure you, you would quickly stop going to him for treatment. But if all these persons are sure and unwavering in word and deed, the self-confidence that they display inspires you with immediate trust.

The great generals are invariably those who are convinced they will win. Do you suppose that soldiers, who must stake their very lives upon the consequences of their chief's decisions, will fight victoriously for a man who only half-heartedly believes that his tactics will bring victory? At the start of a battle, a commanding officer always issues an order of the day in which he states his certainty of victory; he knows well that this will breathe confidence into his troops and make them put forth their best efforts.

When election time comes, never do we fail to hear the heads of opposing political parties declare that they are sure to win. Each is aware that if he seems doubtful, the voters will flock to the banner of the other party's candidate.

Knute Rockne, the famous coach of the football team of the University of Notre Dame, is gone, but he is not forgotten; the spirit of a man is much more durable than the flesh. At the start of a football season, an inquirer once asked Knute to predict for him how many games the Notre Dame team was going to win that year. Knute's answer was simple but memorable: "We are planning to win them all." That was the spirit of a winner. It entered into the blood of his team, released energies they did not know they possessed, and often carried them to victory over forbidding odds. That spirit must be yours in everything you do.

Doubt destroys. Faith builds. If you act as though you could not possibly fall short of your goal, then you will not. This is the rule on which the masters of the earth have molded their lives.

Booker T. Washington Knew the Secret

The further a person plans to go in life, the greater is the requirement that he believe in himself. Few have had to overcome more handicaps than Booker T. Washington, outstanding Negro teacher and reformer, yet everything was possible for this man of intense faith.

Washington was born a slave, the lowest of the low. Emancipation, when it came, was a good thing, but it did not substantially improve his condition; after the Civil War he gained a meager livelihood by laboring at a salt furnace and later in a coal mine. His early education he had acquired at night, while employed as a house servant. Now, hungry for more learning, he cheerfully walked and hitchhiked five hundred miles to a high school, where he earned his keep by working as a janitor. Ultimately he achieved his goal—he earned a certificate permitting him to teach. He had never doubted that he would make the grade, and now he was launched on the route to success!

In the years that followed, Booker T. Washington taught—and he studied too, for he was not a man to be satisfied with things as they were. While he was still in his early twenties, his knowledge and ability brought him recognition; he was named organizer and principal of a new teachers' college for Negroes at Tuskegee, Alabama. The school, started in a small church and shanty, soon grew in size and reputation. Under Washington's confident guidance, in time it became one of the finest colleges in the South. A President of the United States was proud to call him his friend. Harvard and other universities vied with one another in conferring honorary degrees upon this willing worker whose rise from slavery to eminence as an educator became known throughout the world.

How did Booker T. Washington manage to do it,

when millions of his fellows ended their lives in the same humble surroundings in which they were born? Can you guess the secret that made this achievement possible for him, when thoughts of failure, poverty and inferiority froze so many others in their tracks? Let him reveal it to you in his own words, written as he glanced retrospectively over the difficult years:

"I will not say that I became discouraged, for as I now look back over my life, I do not recall that I ever became discouraged over anything I set out to accomplish. *I have begun everything with the idea that I could succeed,* and I never had much patience with the multitudes of people who are always ready to explain why one cannot succeed."

How Failure Thoughts Harm You

Nothing brings on failure so swiftly and surely as fear of failure. If you are afraid you will not succeed, you become tense, and unable to use your natural abilities in the relaxed manner that allows them to come into full play. For proof of this, watch a child learning to catch a ball. If he has not been suitably encouraged in the earliest stages, he doubts his ability to close his hands on it. He is so nervous that he brings his hands together before the ball is between them; he overreaches or underreaches. Lacking confidence in his ability, he is even afraid of the ball itself. When it comes near, he shuts his eyes and the ball, practically within his grasp, goes flying past.

Anyone can catalogue other examples of the damaging effects of self-doubt. Says Professor Joseph Jastrow, one of America's leading psychologists:

"When about to jump a ditch, your confidence that

you can make it helps you to jump farther. Any serious
doubt or hesitation may be conveyed to your muscles
and land you in the mud just short of the bank. In
these matters, thinking things so helps to make them
so."

Faith, it has been said, can move mountains. It
doesn't do this by magic. It does do it, however, by
permitting men to use their ordinary abilities to the
fullest degree possible. Most men do not realize what
impressive things they are capable of, simply because
they lack the confidence to try.

TRAITORS WITHIN

Doubts about your abilities and your future are your
worst enemies. To you as an individual, they are as
dangerous as is a fifth column to your country. They
can undermine your will to succeed unless you are constantly on the alert for them, and deal with them
decisively and intelligently.

It never pays to close your eyes to reality. In any
endeavor, doubts—the traitors within—are certain
to appear, and it is a grievous error to make believe
they are not there. These enemies will try to pass
themselves off as friends. They will pose as legitimate
criticisms of your schemes, as sensible questionings of
the worth of your ideas. But when you scrutinize them
closely, nine times out of ten you will perceive under
these disguises your old foes: the poverty thought, the
failure thought and all their menacing fraternity.
Counter these illusions with Contrary Concentration.
After a while, as you grow in confidence, they will
know better than to seek to infiltrate your mind.

YOUR OPPORTUNITIES

One especially harmful doubt you will encounter concerns not your abilities but your opportunities. This brother of the failure thought will suggest, oh so plausibly and convincingly, that the chance of getting ahead is today slimmer than it ever was before. All the fortunes have been made, this doubt will whisper to you insidiously; all the seats at the table of prosperity are taken, and you would be smart to content yourself picking the small bones of the paltry meal that fortune has served you.

Know your enemy, the disarming falsehood, and know your friend, the invigorating truth. There is still plenty of room at the top. Opportunity always exists for the man or woman who has the imagination to see it—*and the confidence to seize it!*

In a typical week, the United States Patent Office issued five or six hundred patents: The total number issued to date is close to three million. Thousands of these have brought enormous wealth to their owners: average people who had the good sense to recognize a good idea when it presented itself to them.

In other fields, the record is the same. In good times and bad, each decade new fortunes are built, and enterprising persons that no one ever heard of before gain riches and renown. *Why not you?*

IDEAS PLUS CONFIDENCE

Constructive ideas, inspired by confidence in your future, should be your stock in trade. By all means, put them to the test—convince yourself of the merit of your schemes so that all doubts will be excluded—and then go ahead with all your might. They may be small ideas, for improving efficiency in your office or your business, or larger ones for bringing in more income. Once you have assured yourself of the worthwhileness of your plans, you will not find it hard to persuade other people to go along with you in support of them. *First and foremost, however, you must believe in your ideas yourself.*

If you want to amass a fortune, you must believe implicitly that fortunes can still be made. Tell this to yourself often in your Contrary Concentration; tell yourself, too, to be always on the watch for practical, constructive ideas.

Despite the ill-founded opinions of cynics, no area of human needs or interests has a limit to its development. Take travel as an illustration. Man traveled exclusively by foot once, until the creative thinkers of prehistoric times saw the possibilities of easier transportation in taming horses, in building boats and wagons. These great strides forward were only the beginning of the things human ingenuity was to achieve. Other thinkers, when man moved into the age of mechanical power, devised trains that were moved by steam engines and electric engines; the automobile and the airplane were created. Inventive minds projected improvements of the old type of airship into reality—the jet-propelled airplane and the helicopter dominate the skies today, and new wonders are certain to appear tomorrow.

For the creative thinker with confidence, there are infinite possibilities. They are all about him, waiting to be believed in and developed. As Ralph Waldo Emerson has said:

"And what if trade sow cities
Like shells along the shore,
And thatch with towns the prairie broad
With railways ironed o'er?—
They are but sailing foam-bells
Along Thought's causing stream,
And take their shape and sun-color
From him that sends the dream."

A Mother's Idea Makes a Fortune

There is no telling where you will find the idea that will make your fortune. Somewhere, this minute, the conditions needed to produce it already exist. With alertness, you will surely find it. Keep your eyes open for it all the time. Fasten them on the obvious things —the things so close to home that no one looks at them any more. That is what Mr. and Mrs. Dan Gerber did, and they aren't sorry.

The name of Gerber is famous today for the excellent line of baby foods on which it appears. The Gerber Products Company, in recent years, has had sales in excess of $75,000,000 a year. Yet in 1927 Gerber's Baby Foods was only an idea in the minds of Mr. and Mrs. Dan Gerber—an idea they had faith in.

How did the idea come to them? One evening Mr. Gerber arrived home from work in the family cannery, then known as the Fremont Canning Company and noted principally for its tomato purees. Mrs. Gerber had been laboring hard that hot day, under instructions from her family physician to prepare special light, nourishing foods for her baby daughter. Why, Mrs. Gerber asked her husband, couldn't his cannery strain some vegetables other than tomatoes, for small children to eat? And some fruits as well? Mothers, she assured him out of her own bitter experience, would welcome them.

Her suggestion made sense to Dan Gerber. At the cannery, during the following weeks, he strained vegetables and brought them home. Mrs. Gerber was delighted with their taste and texture. The baby's appetite for the new foods showed that she shared her mother's opinion. With this encouragement, Dan Gerber went ahead and formed the Gerber Products Company to produce and market these novel foods.

It soon became apparent that what one mother and baby liked, thousands of others did, too. Mr. Gerber proceeded to expand his list of products. The modest $40,000 advertising budget he started with in 1928 had jumped to $125,000 by 1935 (a depression year). Today Gerber's can proudly say that it spends more than $2,000,000 a year in advertising—and every one of these dollars brings in close to forty more in sales! The company, a leader in its field, has approximately seventy baby food products, which it sells throughout the world.

Mr. and Mrs. Gerber can well congratulate themselves that they had faith in an idea.

Three Young Men with a Notion

Maybe you have never heard of Whitney Miller, Robert W. Gibson, and David M. Lilly. Their names are not so well known outside their own field, it is true—but the organization they have developed, the Toro Manufacturing Corporation, which produces lawn mowers, has rolled up a tidy little sales record of better than $10,000,000 a year for the last few years! These bright young men went into business at the end of World War Two, when they were all under thirty. To get started, they had to borrow money—lots of it. But that did not disturb them, for they had faith in their venture.

No doubt you remember the time when lawn mowers were driven by hand—it was not so long ago. Later, power-driven mowers made their appearance, but these machines were employed chiefly on sizable estates and golf courses. Inevitably this idea had to appear: Why not produce a motorized lawn mower for the homeowner? That notion seems a very obvious one now, but it was a novelty when it occurred to Messrs. Miller, Gibson, and Lilly. Careful investigation showed them that there would be a demand for such a product.

The going was not easy when these young men produced their first motor-driven machines. Factory engineering was not quite perfect, and serious technical problems had to be solved. Patience and confidence brought the solutions, however. New ideas created new products. The Toro owners developed a leaf-mulcher attachment for their mower that would permit it to mulch leaves in autumn as well as cut grass in the summer months. Sales shot up thousands of per cent as this practical inspiration reaped its inevitable reward.

How to Strengthen Your Faith

Merely to look at the achievements of these persons and thousands like them should fill you with confidence in the promise the future holds for you. When doubts arise to worry you, it is comforting to remember the successes of the past, and to realize that still greater ones are possible in the years that lie ahead. This was suggested earlier in our discussion of Contrary Concentration; it is recommended by many authorities, ancient and modern.

"Is example nothing?" asked Thomas Burke, famed eighteenth-century English legislator and author. "It is everything. Example is the school of mankind, and they will learn at no other." Burke's favorite motto was: "Remember—resemble—persevere."

The Masters of the Far East, stalwart as they are in faith, learn to augment their powers still more by emulating the yogis of old. They strive to model themselves after the great teachers of their tradition, such as Buddha, the Enlightened One. You, too, will gain in self-confidence and capability by following this practice.

Human beings are by nature imitative. All the worthwhile things that we know—even our goals in life—we learn, consciously and unconsciously from those we esteem: first, from our parents, then our teachers and friends, later, from admired ones of our own choosing. The finer the models we select for ourselves, the higher will be our accomplishments.

Study well the lives of those whom you would like to resemble. There are available today hundreds of biographies, memoirs, diaries, and collections of the letters of persons who have succeeded in every field. By reading these books, not only will you gain a liberal education in many subjects and a wider understanding of human nature, but you will also acquire the very attitudes and ways of meeting new situations that were so helpful to your models. You can learn the words your heroes spoke, even their innermost thoughts, and make these your own. By building a bookshelf of your favorite great lives—Carnegie, Lincoln, Roosevelt, Peary, Edison, or anyone else—you can have them constantly at your side, to guide, admonish, and inspire you. Just the sight of the books themselves will add fuel to the fire of your ambition.

Pictures of great men and women are another source of encouragement. If you aspire to be a captain of industry, frame on your walls the photographs of men like Firestone, Chrysler, Ford, or Rockefeller. If you want to be an inventor, put up the likenesses of Edison, Watt, McCormick, Marconi, or Morse. If you seek renown as a writer, you will find it stimulating, when you glance up from your work, to look into the eyes of Ernest Hemingway, Willa Cather, Browning, or Shakespeare.

Choose the Right Friends

To build your self-confidence, you should associate with persons who are encouraging to you. Common sense dictates that you should stay away from those who take a perverse delight in pointing up your shortcomings or supposed weaknesses in your plans. A realistic person will always welcome well-informed, constructive criticism, but when an individual consistently belittles you or your ideas, you will be wise to shun him. Probably he behaves this way because in proportion as he diminishes your stature he rises in his own opinion. You can find plenty of honest people who are in sympathy with your projects and whose companionship gives your spirits a lift.

"Keep good company, and you shall be of the number," wrote George Herbert. It is most important to be friendly with people who are interested in the same goals you are. If you do not know such persons, you can meet them readily enough in professional groups or trade organizations. There are associations of salesmen, mail-order people, printers, artists, and persons engaged in almost every other kind of activity.

In spending his time with persons who have similar interests, a man learns new ideas. In matching his wits with those of others like himself, he gains a truer measure of his abilities, is spurred on to higher achievement, and grows in self-confidence. If you cannot locate a suitable organization, but are acquainted with several people possessing ambitions like your own, perhaps you can form your own group.

Find Encouragement When You Need It

Another extremely effective device for generating self-faith is to keep a notebook of inspiring sayings and poems, and look at them constantly until you know them by heart. Should dark moments come when you doubt your future, you will find that these quotations will give you fresh courage.

People of all colors and creeds draw comfort and courage from inspirational writings. The Buddhist reminds himself of his control over his destiny by repeating to himself Buddha's moving admonition: "Rouse thyself, examine thyself by thyself, thus self-protected and attentive wilt thou live happily! For self is the lord of self, self is the refuge of self." The Christian casts out his worries about the future by calling to mind the words of Jesus: "Wherefore, if God so clothe the grass of the field, which today is, and tomorrow is cast into the oven, shall he not much more clothe you, O ye of little faith?" In time of trouble, people have always turned to the Scriptures for consolation.

One eminently successful man I know—he is the founder and owner of a large typewriter sales agency and repair service—has learned by heart an almost incredible number of poems and Bible passages. When his plans go awry, he recalls an appropriate saying to remind himself that there is always "a budding morrow in midnight." Immediately dark thoughts are scattered and his perspective is restored, so that he can move forward again.

I can recall visiting this man over twenty years ago, when he was a struggling young mechanic. In a corner of his mirror, I noticed an inspiring poem he had pasted there; he told me that, when he brushed his hair in the morning, his eyes could not miss this poem, and reading it heartened him for the day's difficulties. Several of his favorite poems were framed neatly on the walls of his bedroom. Never have I known a cheerier, friendlier, or more ambitious person, I do not doubt that these verses helped to make him so.

It is not for nothing that every great family of the past—the ruling houses of Germany, France, England, and Spain and their noble retainers—has always had its inspirational motto. Sir Philip Sidney, who represented the flower of England's manhood in Elizabethan days, selected for himself a truly fine one: *"Viam aut inveniam aut faciam"*—"I will find a way or make one." A large American college has another splendid motto: *"Per aspera ad astra"*—"Through hardships to the stars." Everyone knows the motto of the United States Marines: *"Semper fidelis"*—"Always faithful." The leathernecks have never been false to their motto, to no small degree because they see it constantly, and it reminds them of the high standards they have set for themselves. You, too, will draw courage and heightened self-faith from the mottos and poems that you select to set a standard for your aspirations and the way you go about making them into a reality.

> "There is no great and no small
> To the soul that maketh all;
> And where it cometh, all things are;
> And it cometh everywhere.
> I am the owner of the sphere,
> Of the seven stars and the solar year,
> Of Caesar's hand, and Plato's brain,
> Of Lord Christ's heart, and Shakespeare's strain."

CHAPTER IX

THE FIFTH SECRET

If anything is to be done, let a man do it, let him
attack it vigorously! A careless pilgrim only scatters
the dust of his passions more widely.

—BUDDHA

Some people suppose that the Masters of the Far East
care nothing for action. Those who do not know the
Masters often picture them as mild, contemplative
creatures whose only interest is meditation, in which
they seek an understanding of the hidden truths of life.

This, however, is only one side of the coin. Many
of the seers of India and China have been men of
action. They have lived not in caves, but among people,
and through their energetic efforts have changed the
daily habits and destinies of nations.

Confucius, for all his devotion to wisdom, took an
active part in government. Like Jesus, who followed
him five hundred years later, Buddha placed his emphasis upon communion with God—but he never ceased
from traveling and preaching, trying to get people to
change their self-centered outlook and raise their
moral standards. And Mahatma Gandhi? Although
much of his life was spent in fasting and prayer, for

over fifty years he labored day and night, writing and speaking, organizing meetings and mass action, to mobilize his people's sentiment so they would unite and resist the will of their oppressors. This frail little yogi, more than any other single individual, was responsible for the liberation of a nation of 400,000,000 people from British rule.

Mahatma Gandhi, like all of the other Masters of the Far East, was a godly man. Like them, he knew the secrets of getting what he wanted. Having faith in yourself, and strengthening your one-pointedness by prayer and Contrary Concentration are two of these secrets. Knowing your goal, visualizing it concretely, and moving toward it step by step, while you act as though you could not fall short of it—these are other secrets you must master if you wish success in life's endeavors.

But there is still another secret. If you do not know it—if you do not practice it—you will accomplish only a small portion of the great things that lie within your power.

The Law of Achievement

We can find a clue to this secret in a thin little volume that Mahatma Gandhi never tired of reading. It is one of the Sacred Books of the East and its name is the *Bhagavad Gita,* or *Celestial Song.* Says this ancient book: "No one has attained his goal without action." Elsewhere in it we encounter these words, which, it is worth noting are spoken by a god: "Those who long after success in action on earth worship the shining ones; for in brief space, truly, in the society of men, success is the outcome of action."

The Masters of the Far East glorify action, even when they are speaking of spiritual effort. Patanjali, whose aphorisms inspire so many millions of seekers after the truth in India, declared: "Success is speedy for the extremely energetic."

In thought or deed this is the law: *The more energy you expend, the more impressive will be your victory.*

ENERGY, THE ESSENCE OF SUCCESS

Energy is of the essence of success. Action—unceasing action—is one of the cardinal secrets of achievement. Consider the career of any great or successful man, and the first trait you will be struck by is his inexhaustible energy.

He has realized that the hours are precious—that even a few moments invested to good purpose will do more for him in the end than days and months spent in idleness or transitory pleasures. He knows that worthwhile things require time and effort.

Look at the eminent men of science and industry. Edison, for one, said: "I never did anything worth doing by accident, nor did any of my inventions come by accident." He did not invent the electric light, the phonograph, moving pictures, or his scores of other creations through random experiments, but only after years of intensive work and research. Charles Kettering and his staff at General Motors did not develop an efficient gasoline engine by daydreaming. They worked ceaselessly for more than thirty years before they succeeded in producing the mechanism they wanted.

The Mayo brothers became great doctors not just through native skill, but also because they painstakingly studied new developments in their field of medicine. They never tired of seeking out other physicians and learning from them the better techniques these physicians had evolved for treating the maladies of mankind.

Men of Great Achievement

Look at the great men of music. All were persons of extraordinary energy. Haydn composed a hundred and six symphonies, two hundred concertos, eighty-three violin quartettes, sixty sonatas, fifteen masses, fourteen operas and scores of other pieces. You could not call him an idler, could you?

Georg Friedrich Handel was a constant and rapid worker, even after he had been partially disabled by paralysis. He had a favorite harpsichord, every key of which, by incessant practice, was hollowed out like the bowl of a spoon. *The Messiah* was executed by him in twenty-three days, and *Israel in Egypt* in twenty-seven. In one year he composed *Saul, Israel, Dryden's Ode, Jupiter in Argos* and his *Twelve Grand Sonatas*—all first-rate works.

But Mozart was still more rapid and energetic. His *Marriage of Figaro* was composed within a month, the grand finale of the second act occupying him two nights and a day, during which he wrote without intermission. *Don Giovanni* was composed in six weeks, after the whole subject had been thoroughly digested in Mozart's mind. The overture was not begun until the night previous to that fixed for the first performance of the opera. He began it about midnight, and it was ready in the morning.

The Magic Flute also was written with extraordinary energy. Mozart worked at the opera night and day, and finished it in a few months. Like the two operas just mentioned, it is among the greatest of all musical compositions.

THE BEST PRODUCE THE MOST

Our great writers, like our musicians, have been men of surpassing energy. As Robert Southey said, "The best artists—have produced the most." William Shakespeare wrote ceaselessly; his work is as remarkable for its quantity as it is for its quality. Mark Twain's collected works fill more than twenty volumes. So do the novels and plays of Honoré de Balzac, the writings of George Eliot, and Charles Dickens.

"THERE IS A MAN!"

Or take Johann Wolfgang von Goethe, universally recognized as the most outstanding man of letters that Germany has ever produced. He wrote hundreds and hundreds of poems; many are so lovely that Schumann and Schubert and other famous composers set them to music, and every German knows and sings them. He turned to fiction, and one distinguished novel after another came from his pen. Goethe's restless genius was attracted to science, where his fertile imagination divined many truths so far ahead of his time that they could not be verified until a hundred years later, in our own day, by experiments conducted in modern laboratories. He wrote a large number of plays (his *Faust* is the most famous) that have become a part of the world's literary heritage.

It is not surprising that Bonaparte, when he traveled through Germany, made a point of calling on Goethe at Erfurt. After their meeting, the only words the

French emperor could think of to describe his reaction to this prodigy of energy were *"Voilà un homme!"* ("There is a man!")

What Is Genius?

Well, you may say, all this is very inspiring, but these were no ordinary men. How can I, merely through effort, hope to accomplish what they did? After all, they were geniuses!

Genius can mean many different things. What, however, does it mean to the geniuses themselves? Fortunately some of them, in widely different fields, have set down their conception of genius.

According to Thomas Carlyle, who was an acknowledged genius of literature, history, and philosophy, "Genius is an infinite capacity for taking pains."

Of his own brilliant talent for statecraft and finance, Alexander Hamilton, one of our Founding Fathers, said, "All the genius I have is merely the fruit of labor."

Ignace Paderewski, great as a statesman and a pianist, declared, "Before I was a genius I was a drudge."

Michelangelo, whose statues represent the glory of Renaissance art, had a thought on this subject much like the rest. To those who admired his sublime achievements he confided, "If people knew how hard I labor to get my mastery, it would not seem so marvelous after all."

Gustave Flaubert, one of the immortals of French literature, summed it up this way: "Genius, in the phrase of Buffon [a famous French naturalist], is only long patience." And Flaubert added one word of advice to those who want to be considered geniuses. He said: "Work."

Did Flaubert know what he was talking about? No one could have known better. Every word this genius penned was written in an ink of which the major ingredient was perspiration. It was Flaubert's practice to lock himself in his study and write and rewrite ceaselessly, year after year. So high was his standard that often, at the end of a day's labors, he had produced only a single paragraph. But, because of the pains he took, his books are masterpieces of the French language. They will be read so long as there is a Frenchman alive to read them.

EMERSON'S FORMULA

What, essentially, makes some men stand out more than others? Emerson, a student of the Oriental Masters and a fountainhead of perceptive thought in his own right, gives us a further helpful insight into this matter of success. He says: "A man is like a bit of Labrador spar, which has no luster as you turn it in your hand, until you come to a particular angle, then it shows deep and beautiful colors. There is no adaptation or universal applicability in men, but *each has his special talent, and the mastery of successful men consists in adroitly keeping themselves where and when that turn should be oftenest to be practiced."*

In a few words: In order to win worldly success you must be able to do at least one thing better than other men—but you must do that one thing repeatedly, at the right time and in the right place.

Almost everybody has his special talent. As suggested in our chapter on choosing your goal, your main activity in life should be the thing you like to do best, the career or pursuit you have selected for yourself. The only question is: Is your special talent special enough to win you success? If it isn't, how can you make it so?

Before any talent can blossom, it has a lot of growing to do. That is the way it was with one of the greatest talents of all—William Shakespeare.

Shakespeare was no world-famous genius when he first took pen in hand. Such plays as *Hamlet* and *The Tempest* were the creations of his mature years. Before he became capable of producing those masterpieces, he wrote a long series of mediocre poems and plays. He began by rewriting old potboilers that the theater employing him wanted freshened up. His hand gained in skill as he worked on these drab blood-and-thunder dramas, which today are known only to scholars and theatrical critics. He served as an actor too (they say he played an excellent ghost in *Hamlet*), which gave him practical understanding of the requirements of a good play. He stuck to his job indefatigably, and the longer and harder he worked, the better a playwright he became. Through energetic action, he developed his special talent.

THE SECRET OF MASTERY

Like Shakespeare, *the more you do, the more you will become capable of doing.* It is practice and experience that make the expert. Perfection is no hothouse flower that can be forced into bloom overnight. It is only by laboring as hard as you can, day by day, that you can improve your ability and move closer to your goal.

148

You cannot work toward the fulfillment of your ambitions by fits and starts. You must keep constantly active, steadily bettering yourself, if you hope to get concrete results. Achievement has a direction—it goes uphill; relax your efforts and you will slide back.

Paderewski, the famed Polish pianist whom we have already quoted, once declared: "If I miss practice one day, *I* can notice the difference in my playing; if I miss two days, my *critics* notice the difference; and if I miss three days, my *audience* notices the difference."

GIVE YOUR BEST

It isn't sufficient merely to be energetic; you must be as energetic as you can, and put forth the best efforts that are in you. Patanjali says in his sutras that the success of aspirants "differs according as the means they adopt are mild, medium, or intense." Don't be satisfied to give to your endeavors merely a portion of what is in you. It is only by giving more than enough that you can be sure you are giving the amount that is required for success.

There are enormous powers of achievement sleeping within you—even the seeds of greatness, we said in an earlier chapter. They are waiting to be awakened and brought to blossom. Give more than enough, and you will find out what you are truly capable of.

"Surely," said Woodrow Wilson, "a man has come to himself only when he has found the best that is in him, and has satisfied his heart with the highest achievement he is fit for. It is only then that he knows . . . what his heart demands." By a maximum effort today, you prepare yourself for the greater achievements of tomorrow. Each time you exert yourself more than you did previously, you ascend to a higher level of creativity, performance, and self-fulfillment.

Your Lost Heritage of Power

Nature teaches us that it is more normal to be energetic than to be idle or lazy. Activity is a quality of life.

At birth, you were extremely energetic. You kicked and cried until you were worn out. As an infant, you ceaselessly explored your surroundings, feeling, poking, manipulating, crawling. Each new experience provoked you to new action: everything you saw or heard stimulated and excited you. The more you did, the more your understanding and ability expanded. It looked as though there could be no limit to your development.

Then a misfortune befell you. As you grew out of childhood, you began to lose these wonderful, God-given qualities of energy and interest. The "distorted pictures" of which the yogis speak began to take hold of your mind. You convinced yourself that you had to be bored, poor, weak, or mediocre; that effort did not pay. The magnificent power of mental growth you were born with withered and shrank like an unused limb.

But now, realizing that success is for the energetic —that in many instances energy is the most essential part of genius—you must cast your apathy aside. Sloughing off the husk of false inhibiting images, you must rediscover within yourself the long-dormant creative energy of the Universe and put it to work for you. When an opportunity to better yourself is presented, you must seize it without delay, for it will not tarry. As a sage of bygone years expressed it: "The passing moment is an edifice which the Omnipotent cannot rebuild."

IDEAS ARE OPPORTUNITIES

Ideas, too, are opportunities. It is a fact that they won't keep. When they arise in your mind, they glow with a white heat. Don't minimize your constructive thoughts or allow them to fade into limbo. When you get an idea, write it down without delay. As soon as you can, come back to it, and screen it carefully. You will find that many of your ideas stand up, and that you should do something about them. Be like Faraday, the great English scientist, of whom Tyndall said, "In his warm moments he formed a resolution and in his cool moments he made that resolution good."

An awareness of the value of ideas—that unless they are seized they may escape forever—has been a characteristic of many great men. That was certainly true of Goethe. People often commented on the fact that when they were with him, engaged in an interesting conversation, suddenly a bemused look would come over his face, he would excuse himself and go into another room: an idea had just struck him, and he could not wait to put it down on paper. Alexander Pope, a distinguished English poet, used to keep writing materials close by his bed, so that he could make a note of any thought that came to him while he was lying down. The famed musician Beethoven always carried a notebook with him, and jotted down in it any themes for musical compositions that entered his mind when he was away from home. His notebooks still exist, and in them may be found the germinal ideas for many pieces that he later developed and made great.

J. B. Priestley, one of the most successful of contemporary writers, also keeps such a notebook. He tells us:

"I try to make a note of an idea when it first occurs to me . . . As a rule if it is a good idea I do not need to find it in my notebook: it stays in my mind, and keeps worrying me. But there are notable exceptions. A play that has been successfully performed in about fifteen countries (and is now a film), *An Inspector Calls,* was based on an idea that had been hiding in my notebook for years."

GIVING DIRECTION TO MENTAL ENERGY

Ideas are the products of mental energy. Mental energy is as real as physical energy, and even more basic, since it triggers your actions. Don't ever waste your mental energy when you can be using it to enrich yourself.

Perhaps you have to travel to and from work every day. You may ride twenty or thirty minutes in a train or a bus, each way. As you look about you on this journey, you will notice some people reading newspapers, magazines, or paperback novels; others are sleeping, lost in reverie, or simply looking curiously at the faces and clothing of those who sit opposite. Virtually all are engaged in discharging mental energy in one way or another—*but most are wasting this priceless vital force which could be working constructively for them.*

While you are sitting in the train or bus, or whenever you have free moments, give your mental energy direction. If you are a teacher, you can plan or search for new ways to stimulate your pupils and make them learn better. If you are a salesman, you can think systematically of new ways to sell your merchandise, or of new outlets that might be interested in it. If you are a writer, you can figure out a plot for your next story. If you are going abroad on a business trip next year, you can open a textbook and study the language of the people you have to deal with. If you are a manufacturer, you can use free moments to think up new products.

In a year, twice twenty minutes a day (going and coming from work) adds up to a sizable number of hours. Those hours, spent in constructive concentration, can mean problems solved, valuable knowledge mastered, good planning that will make you more effective as an individual. It should not take long to translate this into a promotion, a raise in pay, or increased income acquired in other ways.

It's all very well to rest your mind when you are tired, but often you are not nearly so tired as you imagine. By a mental effort—an effort of the will, if you prefer—you can cast out the fatigue impression, and make your mind buckle down to the task. Don't drift idly with the current of your reverie; instead, make your thoughts go where you want them to. Center them upon some problem or some subject that is important to you. Use your mental energy to some good purpose. Carry a pad with you, and jot down any thoughts that come to you enroute.

Think It, Do It

When you get a constructive idea, don't be satisfied merely to write it down or to talk about it. Pursue it energetically. Many of your thoughts call for immediate action. Get going, and see what you can make of your idea.

Some of the most successful business executives I know follow this policy. When they think of doing a thing, they do it at once. If they have a project they want to submit to someone, they don't file it away for correspondence a few days later; instead, they get right on the telephone and call the person they want to speak to, even though he is at the other end of the continent. This way, they start the ball rolling sooner and get results much more quickly.

Light Your Own Fires

Another important quality of successful people is their capacity for lighting their own fires. If things are going well for them, they are not content to stand by and wait until adversity summons them to exert themselves On the contrary, they are always seeking ways and means of improving their position, and at no point more than when the world might expect them to be complacent. They know that things will not stay the way they are. Conditions are always changing, and if we do not take an active part in controlling their direction, the change may be for the worse. Most smart business men guide themselves by this rule.

"Unless we keep on developing and marketing new products, we know we will run into old age and attrition," says Lewis E. Phillips, president of National Presto Industries, Inc. "We are determined not to have this happen."

In just a single year, Mr. Phillips has revealed, his organization has chalked up close to $50,000,000 in sales. Still, this enlightened executive knows that he cannot expect such success to continue without new, aggressive effort.

Presto is known throughout the country for the excellent pressure cooker it produces. But it has branched out into other, related fields. It makes heavy cast aluminum cooking utensils, an electric skillet, an electric deep fryer, the Martin outboard motor, a steam electric iron, and a variety of other products. All the same, Mr. Phillips says Presto is bent upon finding new things to make and tapping virgin markets, while it also works at improving the products already in its catalogue.

I know one manufacturer who is the envy of all who are acquainted with him. He is still under forty years of age, yet has been a leading figure in his field for over a decade. He has made a fortune several times over. All his success is testimony to his ability to light his own fires.

"Personally, I never stop looking for new ideas," he has told me. "I have to keep feeding them into my business constantly. The fact is, the old things get played out sooner or later. One of my products may be going great guns, and then I notice that orders are slackening off. Sometimes I can save the situation by increasing my sales effort or by producing more cheaply, but more often than not I know that the product will never be what it used to be, because of increasing competition. It's time for new ideas, and the more the merrier. The more horses you have in the race, the greater your chance of coming in with a winner.

"In my business, for every product we are selling there are one hundred we are considering and twenty that we are experimenting with or have in various stages of completion. We simply must bring out two or three new things a year if we want to stay in the running."

Keep the Faculty of Effort Alive

So, if you want to get ahead, you should not only be persistently energetic, but you must be a self-starter as well. Keep the faculty of effort alive. Remember that, as the Chinese proverb says, "A journey of a thousand miles begins with but a single step"—and always be ready to take that step and follow it up with many more.

God Helps Those . . .

In all of life's endeavors, it is your own efforts that will help you the most. There are some very fine people who will tell you not to worry about the future —all you have to do is place your faith in God. So you should, but with the complete understanding that God helps those who help themselves. Prayer is extremely effective in aiding you to concentrate and to mobilize all of your energies for a peak effort. Knowing that God is with you is important in striving for success. But it is not fair to expect God to do everything. He expects you to do something, too.

CHAPTER X

THE SIXTH SECRET

Knowing that this body is fragile as a jar, and making thy thought firm as a fortress, thou shouldst attack Mara, the Tempter, with the weapon of knowledge, thou shouldst watch him when conquered, and never rest.

—BUDDHA

Buddha called it Mara, the Tempter. To Patanjali it was maya, or illusion. To Jesus, who wrestled with it for forty days in the desert, it was the devil, or temptation.

Yes, even to great figures like Jesus, Patanjali, and Buddha, temptation came. But not often. They were confirmed in their faith and strengthened by self-knowledge.

With the rest of us—ordinary mortals—the case is far different. The Tempter is always knocking at our doors. More accurately yet, he is our permanent house guest.

If you hearken to temptation often—if you weaken in your desire to project your God-given dreams into reality—instead of coming nearer and nearer as the months and years go by, they will recede further in the distance. They will grow colorless and wispy—remote castles in Spain that you like to dream about, but never really expect to enter and take up residence in.

It is precisely at the moment when you have mastered most of the principles of achievement taught by the Masters of the Far East—when you have found that they work, and you are enjoying the first fruits of success—that you can least of all afford to relax and expect things to continue to go your way.

Remember: Up until now, you have been a creature swayed by circumstances. You cannot expect to change yourself overnight. It takes time and effort to become truly one-pointed. It takes practice to make the principles of achievement a part of yourself.

Only when you have fixed these principles in your subconscious mind and are guided by them with the inflexibility of habit can you hope to enjoy consistent success.

Are You Really Persevering?

Possibly you feel that you are already a paragon of firmness; that you can select your course and then pursue it with great steadfastness. Still, not many people have perseverance sufficient unto their needs. When the going is smooth, one can forge ahead almost without effort—but we can hardly call that perseverance of a high type. It is only when the barometer of circumstance falls, when the tempest howls, and great waves buffet you about, that you give true proof of perseverance by staying on your course and making headway.

Are you really a persevering person in this sense of the word—or do you merely think so? A little self-analysis will reveal the facts.

Look at the quiz that follows. It has been prepared for the purpose of determining your PQ or Perseverance Quotient. There are ten questions, and you should answer them with an honest yes or no if you want to see a true picture of yourself and your powers of perseverance.

1. When you are not tired, do you while away your evenings or other spare time listening to the radio or watching television, although you know there are certain tasks that you should be doing?

2. Do you believe that the man who makes his mark in life does so through skulduggery and deceit, and that only fools work hard?

3. If things go awry, is it your tendency to lay the blame at someone else's door?

4. Do you put away at least a few dollars every week into your savings account, or toward the purchase of a government bond?

5. If you engage in a task and your first efforts prove unsuccessful, do you more often than not give up hope of succeeding?

6. Are you very sensitive to blame or praise or can you accept criticism in good spirit?

7. Do you feel that your employer is completely unappreciative of your efforts, and so put as little of yourself as possible into your job?

8. Do you believe that others are more capable than you and that, try though you may, you will generally fail?

9. When you undertake a task, are you content

to do a mediocre job when, with just a little more work, you could do a fine one?

10. Have you often been called lazy or too easy-going?

What Is Your Score?

If your answer is no to seven or more of these questions, you may congratulate yourself—your Perseverance Quotient is high. If your answer is no to fewer than five of the questions, then your PQ is fairly low, and you had better get busy doing something to raise it.

Whatever your score, it will profit you to read this chapter carefully and take its lessons to heart. They will give you a deeper understanding of the meaning of persistence and show you how to develop it until it becomes second nature with you. Only then will you be one-pointed.

No Rose Without Thorns

The Italians say there is no rose without thorns. Certainly there is no task without its problems. You will find obstacles on the path toward any important goal you have set for yourself—obstacles that you cannot always imagine in advance.

It may happen that an idea that previously inspired you will suddenly appear to require more hard work than you ever imagined. Or your business may require new capital, and you may not know where to find it. Or you may have made some progress with a vital project and then find that certain backers have withdrawn their support. Should you give up? Weary of thinking and trying, dismayed by the magnitude of your problem, it is only natural that you should be tempted to.

At this point, say the Masters of the Far East, your situation might be compared to that of a man who is digging a well. When he starts out, he does not know for sure how long he will have to labor to reach his objective, but, at least at the beginning, he is full of enthusiasm for he pictures his goal very sharply. As he digs, however, he encounters some large boulders. To him they seem gigantic; their removal appears to him a backbreaking task.

The well-digger, like yourself, is caught on the uncommonly sharp horns of a dilemma. If he stops now, he will spare himself the work of lifting the boulders. But with the saving there will be a loss, too —all the labor he has spent in digging will be thrown away. He will not find water.

SOLUTION OF THE MASTERS

For the Masters of the Far East, the dilemma is not difficult to solve. They have a guiding principle of great significance at this juncture. They quote one of their wisest seers, who said: *"It is not the obstacle itself, but the mental picture we have made of that obstacle that dismays us."*

In other words: When we begin to lose heart because of the difficulties that confront us, it is not the difficulties themselves that are the source of our dismay, but the negative way we interpret them.

WHAT OBSTACLES REALLY MEAN

The trials and obstacles that men and women encounter are bad things only if they are viewed that way. The Masters of the Far East have another mode of looking at them. According to their teaching—and it is thoroughly consistent with Christian doctrine—difficulties are meant to stimulate us. They are God's way of making us capable of higher levels of achievement.

When God pits you against a stern adversary, the Masters tell us, He wants you to be the conqueror—but He permits you to succeed through effort and perseverance alone. As you defeat one antagonist after the other, you show yourself to be worthy of greater and greater rewards. If your courage is undaunted, God will grant you your victory.

So here is the way to meet adversaries, obstacles, difficulties, tribulations: Don't be intimidated. Instead, welcome your foes. Roll up your sleeves and prepare to show that you are stronger than they are.

Although the struggle may be no easy one, you may take rich comfort in the thought that, precisely as the rough diamond is polished by friction, so man is made perfect by his trials.

Learn from Your Mistakes

Poets often possess the vision of seers. It was John Keats, one of England's finest poets, who declared: "Failure is in a sense the highway to success, inasmuch as every discovery of what is false leads us to seek earnestly after what is true, and every fresh experience points out some form of error which we shall afterward carefully avoid."

Learn to glean some wisdom from your difficulties and failures. If you do this, each of your errors will contribute to your ultimate success. This is the way of the Masters, and indeed of all whom the world calls great or successful.

It was the way of Ulysses S. Grant, the man who led the Union armies to victory in the Civil War. Before him, there had been other generals in command, yet even with more supplies and manpower than their opponents, they had proved unable to bring the war to a successful close. Grant learned from his predecessors' mistakes. When he made errors, he profited by them. He was perseverance personified.

No doubt we can't all be Ulysses S. Grants, firm in purpose and devout in resolve. Still, like him, through our mistakes we can learn what will serve our purposes and what will not. Through an intelligent observation of our errors, we can become capable of greater achievement.

Don't Give Up the Struggle

The ability to learn from our mistakes is one ingredient of success; unwillingness to give up the struggle when it goes against us is yet another. Indeed, a will of steel will carry a man to the top in the absence of many other desirable qualities. This is shown strikingly by the life of a Russian tyrant born with the name of Djugashvili. This individual was cruel and suspicious by disposition. He lacked both wit and warmth. To make matters worse, he had no faith in God or in his fellow man; sincerity and honesty were missing from his nature. Yet, through the firmness of his will, this man was able to raise himself from a humble cobbler's son to the position of dictator over all the Russians.

The Russians called him the "Man of Steel"— "Stalin," in their language.

It is obvious that if firmness and perseverance can

carry a wicked man so far, these qualities can carry a good man much further. Indeed, if he possesses them, and follows the rules laid down by the Masters, he is fated to rise. If he is deficient in these qualities, if he is easily dissuaded from his purpose, then even the angels themselves could not help him.

Success is not the lot of persons of mediocre staying power. It comes only to those who have more than a fair quota of persistence. The salesman who gives up his efforts to make a sale the moment the customer expresses lack of interest in his product, the advertising man who abandons a well-thought-out promotion campaign when his first ads do not bring results, the storekeeper who is ready to close his new shop if customers do not come flocking in—these have not learned the lesson of persistence and will never garner its rewards.

The man who amounts to something in this life is the one who refuses to take no for an answer. When he encounters opposition, instead of being deterred he redoubles his efforts. Sooner or later, they are crowned with success. All the world loves a lover, but it loves a fighter more.

Persistence Overcomes Refusals

Diogenes, an ancient Greek philosopher, had an instinctive appreciation of this rule. He knew that persistence, if it is exercised for a worthy purpose, can overcome the most stubborn refusal. That is why a story about him comes down to us from old Greece, over the long, dusty span of the two thousand years that separate him from our day.

As a young man, Diogenes had one wish that crowded all others out of his heart. He loved wisdom and he wanted to learn more of it. A leading teacher of philosophy in those times was named Antisthenes, and Diogenes burned with desire to study at Antisthenes' school. Antisthenes had been a pupil of the great Socrates and in his school he taught the Socratic method of attaining virtue by independence and self-control, which closely resembles the method of the Masters of the Far East.

So widespread was Antisthenes' reputation that people came from near and far and begged to be accepted as his disciples. He could not take them all; many had to be turned away. When Diogenes begged the distinguished philosopher to admit him to his school, he was refused.

But Diogenes could not accept defeat. He dogged the older man's footsteps. Wherever Antisthenes went, he saw the imploring face of Diogenes.

Finally Antisthenes showed some most unphilosophic signs of irritation. Was it a ruse—or had he actually lost his famed calmness—when he raised his staff and threatened to strike Diogenes if he did not get out of his way?

"Strike!" was Diogenes' reply. "You will not find a stick hard enough to conquer my perseverance."

But Antisthenes did not strike. Instead, he put down his staff and embraced the young aspirant. Diogenes' determination to study at the philosopher's school had convinced Antisthenes that this was a pupil who would bring credit to his teacher. Nor was the old Greek mistaken in his judgment.

WHY MEN FAIL

Had Diogenes been dismayed by the first refusal, he would never have had an opportunity to realize the ambitions that meant so much to him. But he would not give up. You must show equal, if not greater, determination if you are to get what you want. Aware that fortune favors the persistent, you must stay firm with your desire until it is realized.

In Shakespeare's words: "Do not, for one repulse, forego the purpose that you resolved to effect." In numerous instances, a failure establishes just one fact: your determination to succeed was not strong enough. Most of the things men set their hearts on are not impracticable in themselves. It is for want of perseverance rather than lack of ability, intelligence, or favorable circumstances that men fall short of success.

"WE CAN DO ANYTHING WE WANT TO DO"

"We can do anything we want to do if we stick to it long enough." These simple but profound words were spoken by one of the most extraordinary persons of this or any other time—a woman who was mute but learned to speak; who was blind but learned to know what others saw; who was deaf but learned how to discover what others were saying; who had all these handicaps yet made herself one of the most distinguished authors and most effective humanitarians of our age. The pyramids themselves are not greater monuments of perseverance than her life.

Mark Twain was not exaggerating when he commented that she and Napoleon were the two most interesting persons of the nineteenth century.

Helen Keller became even better known in the twentieth century. An untiring traveler, she found things to see, though she lacked sight. She was received with admiration by the rulers of the world. Her books *The Story of My Life* and *Midstream* were read by millions. Her lectures in many lands created an enlarged understanding of the problems of the sightless, and stimulated the founding of new schools to help them. To the blind themselves she brought a bright new hope for the future.

CHAPTER XI

THE SEVENTH SECRET

Nature is just toward men. She recompenses them for their sufferings; she renders them laborious because to the greatest toils she attaches the greatest rewards.

—MONTESQUIEU

To rise in the world, you must pay the price exacted by the law of achievement. The man who wants to become a general in the Army must put in many more years of application and service than a lieutenant. The captain of a ship earns his post by harder, more responsible work than is performed by the ordinary hand that swabs the decks or toils in the engineroom. The men who dominate the great enterprises of America or who make her laws are no callow youths; effort has etched lines on their faces, and the wisdom of their judgment did not ripen in a year or in a decade.

If you are to make headway in the world, you cannot expect your victories to fall into your lap. You must be prepared to buy them, and to pay for them dearly if necessary. If it is a fortune on which you have set your sights, you should know that you are going to spend hard years of effort laboring for it. While others play, you will have to be working. While others sleep, not only will you have to stay awake—but you will have to be applying yourself almost every moment, often to the limit of your capacity.

If strength of body and good health are the thing you want most in the world, don't think they will come to you as you lie stretched out serenely in a beach chair. The sun will tan you, but it will not build your muscles, firm your back, or strengthen your lungs. Not only will you have to hold the health thought firmly in mind—you will be obliged to spend hours in exercise, each day doing more than you did the day before. It took Theodore Roosevelt years of strenuous application to make himself over from a sickly, puny youth into a forceful, virile man—but he was able to do it because he was prepared to pay the price, although he loved his leisure as much as any man.

If you desire to enjoy social success or public esteem, and that is what you are concentrating on, not only must you be persistent in your concentration—you must get out and move among people constantly. Don't expect them to beat a path to your door simply because you wish it. When you do make friends, you will have to give of yourself in order to keep them. You must enter freely into the give-and-take of friendship, and make the sacrifices that real friendship often requires.

Include Effort in Your Mental Pictures

Always include effort in any picture you form of your goals. Picture yourself working, facing obstacles, and overcoming them. By all means be an optimist, but don't be a foolish optimist—the kind of person that old Chuang Tze, the Chinese sage, described as "one who expects an egg to crow in the morning and hopes to bring down a bird by looking at a bullet."

No, to hatch eggs, you will have to learn modern methods of incubation and follow them faithfully; to bring down a bird, you will have to master, through perseverance, the skills of marksmanship. For any achievement, you must be prepared to pay the price.

Count Your Blessings

When you are low in spirit, or weary of the sacrifices that your goals compel you to make, that is the time not just for Contrary Concentration but for counting your blessings as well. As the child who is saving for some longed-for toy takes his pennies out of his piggy bank now and then and counts them, so you will acquire strength for the hard road you have to travel by pausing to see how far you have come.

Give yourself an accounting of the enterprise to which you are devoting yourself. Allow yourself to see that this month you are further along than half a year ago—that you have gotten a raise or a promotion, and a still better position is open to you in the future. Or that you have saved, though at considerable sacrifice, so many hundreds of dollars, and are closer than ever to the financial security you have been dreaming of. For there is this wonderful thing about labor and perseverance—their fruits are material as well as spiritual, and merely to look at them will hearten you for the efforts that lie ahead.

CHAPTER XII

THE ASANAS—FOR A SOUND BODY

> Whatever position is easy and steady may be considered an asana; that is the sole principle.
>
> —SANKHYA

Up to now, we have placed the accent on mental methods of getting what you want out of life. And properly so, for to the Masters of the Far East the development of the mental powers and the exercise of the spirit are the highest activity of man. At the same time, this does not mean that the yogis belittle the physical side of life. Nothing less than perfection is the aim of yoga—perfection of the body as well as of the mind.

A wise old poet of the Roman Empire once set up as the proper ideal for mankind the development of a sound mind in a sound body. The Masters of the Far East were preaching this doctrine—and practicing it—when great Rome was still a tiny village of straw-thatched huts inhabited by swineherds.

Yoga has a physical code as well as a spiritual one. Lean, intellectual-looking men the Masters of the Far East may be, but they are men for all that—muscular, sound of wind and limb, and capable of remarkable feats of physical stamina. If we were to follow their teachings on body culture, we could enjoy radiant health well into old age, instead of falling off physically, as we usually do, in our middle years or earlier.

It is a common complaint that even before we are forty, most of us begin to sag at the middle. Our abdominal muscles lose their tone, and our joints become stiff and inflexible. If we have to run for a few minutes to catch a train or a bus (this involuntary exercise is the only kind generally practiced in the West by those past twenty-four years of age), our faces turn red, our breath comes short, and our hearts pound like a trip-hammer. Even a long walk is a trial for many of us. After we have gone a few blocks, our aching legs speedily convince us that we are not as young as we used to be.

Civilized man takes better care of his car than he does of his body. He knows perfectly well that if he allowed his car to stand idle or if he neglected it, the battery would run down and the mechanical parts would rust. Periodically he sees to it that the vehicle is greased, the oil is changed, and the motor is given a tune-up so it will be capable of peak performance. But his body? He takes it so much for granted that, except for satisfying his appetite and his thirst, he hardly seems to give his body a thought till he falls ill.

Our moralists like to complain that self-interest rules our lives. Often it does—but just as often it does not. If we were truly self-interested, we would take better care of our bodies.

The truth is that man is a short-sighted creature. He is caught in a trap of his own making, and does not possess sufficient vision to extricate himself. By means of the machines he has invented, he has attained a high standard of living unprecedented in history. But, like anything else in the world, a machine is no better or worse than the intelligence with which it is used. Machines are fine when they produce the good things of life for us. They do us harm when we employ them to such an extent that we allow our own bodies to fall into disuse.

Most Important Machine of All

The body is the most important machine of all. It's far wiser to spend a few minutes a day keeping it in good shape with exercise than to have to spend hundreds of dollars in physicians' fees later on, only to be told that the cure for your troubles is more fresh air—and the exercise you were denying your body in the first place! As the poet Thomson said: "Health is the vital principle of bliss; and exercise, of health."

Strong Body, Strong Will

But the Masters go even further. As they see it, proper body culture is of considerable help in the achievement of yoga. Above all, they are interested in control of the mind so that it will concentrate effectively and do the bidding of the spirit at all times—so that it will be one-pointed, we have said. They feel that the spirit will be all the stronger in concentration if through long practice it has acquired complete command of the body, and every nerve and muscle will do its bidding without resistance.

Simplified Asana Exercises

For the purpose of strengthening the will, the yogis have devised a series of positions or postures in which meditation is to be undertaken. There are eighty-four of these basic postures called asanas (the word, in Sanskrit, means "seats"), and each has an almost infinite number of variations.

To the Oriental the asanas present no special problem, for he has been practicing them from childhood. For Westerners they are often exceedingly difficult without a long period of conditioning to harden the will and the physique.

In the first part of this chapter we shall abstract some of the basic elements of the asanas and present them in the form of simple exercises. Anyone can do these and gain a good measure of the benefit that the authentic asanas bestow upon the yogis. At the end of the chapter, you will find a group of true *yogasanas,* the asanas of the yogis, should you wish to practice them.

Two Values of Asanas

The simplified asana exercises recommended here will have two values for you. The first is physical: these exercises make the body more supple and youthful. Muscles that are in good condition will do more for you when you need them, and give you greater endurance. A number of the exercises are excellent specifics for aches of the neck, shoulders, arms, legs, back, and other parts of the body.

The second value of the asanas is spiritual or mental. Since mind and body are one, the things that are done with the body frequently have an influence on the state of the mind. The yogis are given to practicing several asanas at the start of their meditation or during the course of it. They find that the physical activity relaxes their bodies, clears their minds. As they shift their limbs and exert themselves, the thoughts that earlier preoccupied them fall away and their spirits are refreshed. You are certain to derive some benefit if, like them, you try a few of the simplified asana exercises before you begin your own meditations or Contrary Concentration against the obstacles or weaknesses within yourself that are troubling you.

Most of the exercises recommended here are easy. A few require a fair degree of exertion. You may select whichever ones are best suited to your age and physical condition. For your meditation itself, as suggested in a prior chapter, there is no special asana or position required; the positions assumed for concentration by the yogis would only be distracting for the average American or European. Sankhya, one of the ancient Masters of the Far East, said any posture that is pleasant and steady may be considered an asana; that was the only rule he laid down. Patanjali and other teachers of yogic lore echoed him.

STRENGTH FOR YOUR MIDDLE

Very beneficial to the muscles of the abdomen is a ride on an imaginary bicycle. Swing your legs up in the air so that they are at a right angle to your body. With your elbows resting on the ground, place your hands on your buttocks and grasp them firmly; this will give you support for what is to come. Now move your legs up and down in a rotating motion just as though you were riding a bicycle.

STRENGTHEN YOUR BACK AND NECK

Perhaps you occasionally have reason to complain of aches in your back or neck. If the muscles of these much-neglected parts of the body were stronger, they would not bother you. A helpful technique for imparting strength to the muscles in your back and neck is performed as follows:

Reclining on your bed, turn your hands so that the palms are down. Now, slowly begin to lift your legs as high as you can, pushing upward from the thighs. Bring your legs up and over your head; if your back is flexible, you will succeed in touching your toes to the bed beyond your head. As soon as you have done this, swing your legs back to their original position.

You may not be able to carry this exercise to its proper conclusion at the first try, but it will become easier with practice. Here, as in your other endeavors, you will succeed if you have a will to. The benefits the exercise confers make it well worth the effort required. Actually, to the Masters of the Far East, such an asana is child's play. Many of the Orientals would not think of beginning their day without a setting-up exercise that includes standing on their heads—and suffer no ill effects, even though they are in their sixties or seventies!

If you ever have the opportunity to meet a yogi, one of the first things that will strike you about him is how straight he stands. He may have been on his feet for hours, but you will never see him slouching as we of the West so often do; he carries his head straight and his shoulders are square. On the other hand you won't observe him standing stiff and stern as a tin soldier, either. He holds his head up and his chest high, but he is completely relaxed, for good posture has been a habit with him since boyhood.

Because the yogi stands properly, all of his organs are in a natural, normal position, free of stress or cramping. His spine is as straight as Nature meant it to be, and so he is spared the host of the neck, back, leg, and shoulder pains that Western man has earned as the reward for his highly civilized way of living. In the yogi's relaxed posture and easy manner you see not the remotest sign of nervous tension.

Good posture is not difficult to acquire once you have made up your mind that you desire it. And you owe it to yourself to be concerned about the correctness of your posture, for so much of your physical well-being depends upon it. To find out how good or poor your posture really is, simply get up, go over to the wall, and stand with your heels at the baseboard, your shoulders and buttocks touching the wall. Lean the back of your head against it too. Do you feel any strain when you remain in this position for several moments? If you do, that is proof that your posture is not so perfect as you imagine.

The first step in posture improvement is a mental one. Imprint on your mind the memory of the feeling that you have as you stand upright, in the position just described, against the wall. Later, several times a day, recall the sensation of the wall touching your shoulders, your buttocks, your head. Automatically, you will find that you begin to straighten up, though a little conscious effort may be called for at the start to overcome ingrained bad habits. With your chest up, your shoulders back, your head high, your feet parallel and your knees straight, you will walk better and feel better. Good posture makes for superior physical endurance and a sense of ease and grace as you go about your business.

Good posture is important when you are sitting, too. You can't sit well if you are in an uncomfortable chair, so make sure that the one you use most often is roomy, pleasant to sit in, and not too high or low for your feet to rest easily on the floor. Your spine should be straight, but your posture relaxed, with the massive bones of the pelvic region supporting your trunk as they were intended to. If you sit in an incorrect position, your digestive organs will be cramped and subjected to unnatural pressure, so don't lean far forward, when you are working. Don't cross your legs; this interferes with the circulation of the blood and, if practiced habitually, imposes a strain upon the spine and the muscles of thighs. However, crossing your ankles does no harm.

Now you have the ideal picture of good posture, whether seated or standing. If it is not a faithful portrait of you, there is no need to despair. Anyone can improve his posture. As you sit at a table or at a desk, recall the perfect picture. Try to conform to it. It may not be easy at first, since muscles, like people, get set in their ways. Still, as you practice the asana exercises, you will find that your muscles will become more flexible, and that you can get them to do your bidding without much trouble.

WHY NOT LIVE TO BE 120?

The Yogi has only contempt for our western mode of living. He would not be caught dead eating the foods we eat or treating the body the way we do ours.

The Yogi treats his body with respect, obeying the laws of nature in regards to the body; so that he is never sick and reaches an unbelievable age before he dies. He is active and working up to the last and experiences none of the decrepitude, loss of memory, foggy thinking, and senility which we see in so many aged people today. The Yogi retains his health and strength up to the last and only dies when he has made up his mind that his mission on earth is completed.

Why should we not live at least as long, comparatively, as the animals? The average animal lives to seven times its maturity and retains its vigor and virility until very near the end. Man matures at 18 or 20 years. If he lived as long, comparatively, as the animal, he could expect to reach an age of 126 to 140 years, and to retain much of his youthfulness until very near the end of his days. That much is promised him in the Scriptures. In Job, you find: "His flesh shall be fairer than a child's. He shall return to the days of his youth." Again in Genesis—"And the Lord said, My Spirit shall not always strive with man, for that he also is flesh: Yet his days shall be 120 years."

"For I have no pleasure in the death of him that dieth, saith the Lord; wherefore turn yourselves and live ye!"

Some interesting cases of long life among modern men are here quoted from *The Bionomy of Power,* written and copyrighted by John X. Loughran:

"The record of Li Chung Yen, who recently passed away at the age of 256 years, has been verified by scientific investigators. His four rules for a long life were: Keep a quiet heart, sit like a tortoise, walk sprightly like a pigeon, and sleep like a dog.

"I personally met and interviewed Zora Agha, a Constantinople porter, who at the time had passed 150 years of age. His diet was very simple.

"History abounds in many well-authenticated instances of men and women who retained their health and ability to enjoy life for a very long time. Among women, the most famous is the lovely and romantic Ninon de L'Enclos, enchanting, winning, diaphanously beautiful of face and form. Historians record that even when she was 90 years old, she was so like a beautiful woman of thirty that a young man barely twenty years of age fell hopelessly in love with her. Her diet was simple and abstemious, of dissipation none. Significant in the accounts of her life are the daily periods she devoted to relaxation, simple exercises and the achievement of a serene mental state."

Modern man is beset by thousands of different types of diseases. He blames Heredity, Mother Nature, God, and everything and everybody but himself for the mess he is in. Practically everything civilized man does is wrong, unnatural, disease and death producing. He unwittingly hastens his own burial as fast as he can. His wrong habits are projected into his eating, drinking, breathing, thinking, working, and sleeping. He daily flouts the Laws of God and of Nature and then wonders why he has to pay the penalty.

Medical Science points with great pride to its advances in medicine, surgery, and drugs. But are we really a healthy people? Our doctors are overworked, our hospitals are filled to overflowing. A Medical Survey of Business Executives averaging 44 years of age revealed that fully fifty per-cent of them had ulcers, high blood pressure, or heart disease. During the last war, half of our young men were turned down as physically or mentally unfit for the army. Three out of five men were rejected by the U. S. Navy as unsuitable for service.

Minds and bodies weakened by the ravages of wrong diet and modern living succumb too easily to nervous breakdowns, and in many cases, resulting insanity.

A recent report by the Human Betterment Foundation of Pasadena, California, summarizes statistics regarding insanity as follows: "This, then, is the situation which America faces now: 18,000,000 persons who are or at some time during life will be burdened by mental disease or mental defect, and in one way or another a charge and tax upon the rest of the population. It challenges every thoughtful person. The misery resulting from this insanity and feeble-mindedness provides the first reason for grappling with the problem. No stratum of society is immune from such suffering."

The above facts and figures are quoted by Dr. Carl A. Wickland in his book *The Gateway of Understanding,* published by the National Psychological Institute, Inc., of Los Angeles.

The Science of Yoga can help you to eliminate disease and lengthen your life by many happy years. As a spiritually awakened individual of high mental calibre, it is your beholden duty to God and to your country to live as long as you possibly can. God knows there are far too few of you! The masses of people on earth are wallowing in one huge morass of ignorance and incredible stupidity. Your uplifting influence may help save the world yet!

Yoga Not for the Weak-Willed

Certain books on Arthritis, Cancer, and Heart Disease are very popular today because they appeal to people who are soft, weak-willed, and spineless. They want to be told to eat the things they like and do the things they like to do anyway, and these books do just that. Anything that requires any will power or effort goes against their grain. They are not made of that sterner stuff that characterized our forefathers. Any people who are really cured by the easy methods outlined in these books are probably as scarce as the proverbial hen's teeth.

If you are this type of person, you are wasting your time in reading this book because Yogi takes real effort and time; if only ten minutes a day. However, the rewards for this effort are so amazing and exciting that the results will goad you on to greater efforts and you will find it is really a lot of fun!

Such exercises as the headstand and shoulderstand, described in the chapter, "KUNDALINI YOGA," are of tremendous benefit to the human body. It is claimed that standing on the head or shoulder will erase wrinkles from the face and neck. Yogi students, after a month or two of this exercise, have been accused of going to a plastic surgeon to have their faces lifted. Their friends could not believe that seams and wrinkles had disappeared from doing an exercise! It is also said that these stands will prevent falling hair and greying hair. In fact, grey hair has returned to its former color. This is probably due to the increased circulation of blood in the head.

Pandit Nehru, Prime Minister of India's teeming millions, is probably one of the busiest men on earth. Yet every day, he finds 20 minutes or half an hour to stand on his head! He claims that this adds immensely to his energy and ability to concentrate.

Indra Devi says in her book *Forever Young, Forever Healthy,* published 1954, Prentice Hall, Inc.,

New York; "I am often asked why the yogis pay so much attention to the care of the body when their aim is a spiritual union with the Divine. They keep the body healthy, beautiful, shapely, and clean, within and without, because they regard it as a vehicle through which the Supreme Power manifests Itself. To them the body is a temple of the Living Spirit and, therefore, they believe in bringing it to the highest state of perfection. Just as a violinist, for example, takes great care of his violin, without which he would not be able to express his art, so the yogi takes care of his body, as the only instrument through which he can express his spirituality. It can be said that the practice of Yoga assists the 'Healer,' 'Psychiatrist,' and 'Priest' within us to keep us in physical and mental health and in spiritual awareness."

CHAPTER XIII

BUDDHISM*

Buddha, like many a man before and after him did
not spare himself from any of the impact of man's
ruthless injustice to man and to the abuse of power.
He saw the purposeless sacrifice of the powerless to
human greed. He beheld the inevitable toll of age, sickness and death. Some men, unable to bear this say
"There must be some purpose. Perhaps it is God's
will." But Buddha knew that this did not satisfy him.

Buddha and Christ, living five hundred years apart,
are the two greatest figures of compassion in the
history of the world. Buddha had everything in the
worldly sense, wealth, love, palaces, a son. Jesus had
no place to lay His head.

Buddha was a prince. He had a beautiful wife, a
fine son and every luxury that money could buy. But
he was unable to repress from his consciousness the
knowledge of what other men were going through.
He saw them wasting away with sickness and exhausting toil until they were finally swallowed up by death.
Buddha would not rest until he got to the bottom of
the "tragedy of man."

Once when the rest were feasting perhaps, Buddha
slipped away by himself and wandered toward the
village. There for the first time he saw an aged man,

* *Hindu Philosophy* by Dr. Garabed H. Paelian, published by
Astara Foundation, Los Angeles, California.

a helpless invalid, and a corpse followed by mourners. He was struck anew with the miseries that awaited all that were born. Had the Gods no pity? Life had become a nightmare of horror and injustice to him.

One day when Buddha was 29, he saw a serene figure coming down the road, dressed in a coarse robe of yellow. He carried a bowl in his hand. When the prince looked into the eyes of the sage, he saw a calm face and a soul at rest. Struck by this, the future Buddha asked the august traveler what his mission was.

"Great Lord," the stranger answered, "I am a religious wanderer who, shuddering at the problems of life, seeing all things fleeting, have left the fetters of my home behind to seek some happiness that is trustworthy and imperishable, that looks with equal mind on friend and enemy, and does not regard wealth or beauty. Such is the only happiness which will content me!"

Buddha asked, "And where, O wise man, do you seek it?"

The traveler replied, "Great Lord, in solitude, in the quiet of deep words. There, in the quiet dwells Enlightenment."

Buddha was deeply impressed by these words. From that moment on, he resolved to dedicate himself to a search for the answer to the riddles of Life. That night he quietly slipped away from the life of ease and luxury that he had known for the twenty-nine years of his life. He left his magnificent palace and exchanged his princely trappings for a beggar's robe.

He made his way to a monastery where he studied under the holy men. Although Buddha studied many years and eagerly read everything of Indian Philosophy that had been written up to that time, including the *Vedas* and *Upanishads,* he still was not satisfied that he had solved the Mysteries of the Ages.

Finally, he determined to put to test the Hindu idea that knowledge may be obtained by fasting and the annihilation of all mortal desires. With five companions, he went to a gorge hidden away in the dense jungles of the mountains, there to give himself up to fasting and terrible penances, thinking that he might find the path to enlightenment through pain and suffering. He sat motionless in meditation for such long periods that animals and birds crossed his body.

The fame of this man Buddha soon spread far and wide for he was so engrossed in his aspirations that he ate only a grain of rice a day. People believed that he must be very holy in order to do that and live.

At the end of six years, Buddha had been reduced to a living skeleton and still he had not found the peace of mind that he was searching for. Finally the starvation was more than his frail body could take and he fell unconscious, more dead than alive. When he recovered, the truth became clear to him that salvation lay not in self-torture but in preaching the way of Life to all men.

To the utter dismay of his five companions in fasting, he demanded food. He realized that he would need a healthy body if he wanted to continue living. His companions deserted him, considering him a fallen saint. They renunciated him, believing he was a lost soul and that a thousand fiends would soon fly away with him!

But his years of study and six years of fasting had not been in vain. When his frail body had been restored by food, he resumed his struggle to find his own true nature. He saw a large and broad-leaved Bo tree and sat beneath it in Yoga fashion. He determined never to leave that spot until he had found enlightenment and salvation.

He thought of his wife, his family, his father, his beautiful horse, and his palace. How he was tempted to return to his former life! He was "Jacob wrestling with the angel of the Lord." But he held steadfast to his aims like the arrow seeking its target, and when the darkness thinned, and the east became faintly gray, he received complete enlightenment. Not partial, not intermittent, but clear, steadfast, and perfect. He had attained the highest consciousness and received it with a cry of "Light!"

He beheld the past, present and future as one. He beheld true causation and the secrets of birth and death and the passing on into new lives. He beheld the individuality or ego of man as one with his Divine Parent. And he beheld the Truth, the Way of Escape. Illumined with all wisdom sat the Buddha, the Utterly Awakened, lost in contemplation of the universe as it Is, having entered the Nirvana of peace. At last, he cried aloud in triumph his song of victory,

"Many a house of life
 Has held me, seeking ever that which wrought
 The prison of the senses
 Sorrow fraught
 Sore was my ceaseless strife.
 But now,
 Thou builder of the body prison now
 I know thee! Never shalt thou
 Build again these walls of pain
 Nor raise the roof-tree of deceits nor
 Lay fresh rafters on the clay.

Broken the house is, and the ridge pole split
Delusion fashioned it
Safe pass I hence deliverance to attain."

It was at last not the dewdrop lost in the ocean but the ocean drawn into the dewdrop. Buddha remembered now his past lives and shared in the omniscience of the Infinite.

Buddha was free! He had cried that the mind is not imprisoned by the delusions of the senses and he had found a way of deliverance from pain and sorrow for himself and all mankind. Henceforth he was called "the Buddha," or "the Enlightened One!"

Finding his five companions still torturing themselves, he explained to them what he had learned in that moment of enlightenment; that all suffering came from evil and sensual desires, from greed and selfishness, from a life apart from God. By constant meditation and control of thought, he declared, a habit of thought could be reached in which selfish desires and the mortal will are subdued and communion with one's Divine Nature can be accomplished.

The companions soon saw the light and became his disciples. News of his power and preaching spread like a prairie fire, and multitudes were attracted to him. Even nobles of his former class and station, weary of their endless search for pleasure, gathered unto him, eager to hear of his happiness in the simple, spiritual life.

For those wishing to attain, Buddha described the Noble Eightfold Path.*

The Noble Eightfold Path is "Right Understanding," or realization or recognition of the truth from

* *The Teachings of the Buddhas,* by Dr. Garabed H. Paelian, published by Astara Foundation, Los Angeles, California.

188

illusion. This is the first. The second is "Right Resolution," the will to attain wisdom, once that one has ascertained that such a feat is possible. The third is "Right Speech." This, of course, is not to abuse anyone in any way that breaks the Law of Love. It is, of course, not to lie or employ propaganda to serve personal ends. The fourth is "Right Conduct." Here motive is all. Again, to follow the Law of Love, or the Golden Rule is the only way to escape the prison of Karma.

The fifth is "Right Livelihood." Love and work are the two halves of a man's existence. They can be his prison or his freedom. A man must have his right vocation. Buddha especially indicates that work that causes hindrance to the character of others, like selling alcohol, or that encourages man to destroy his fellow beings (such as munitions making) is immoral.

The sixth is "Right Effort." This is what Seabury calls "a real work habit" as well as a diligent attempt to build an adequate philosophy of life.

The seventh is "Right Meditation." Time to be alone, to think things through and to face courageously that which disturbs is essential for spiritual growth. Its function is also to raise one's sights, to invoke greater understanding from the infinite mind.

The eighth is "Right Rapture." This is happiness right here on this earth. It is the peace that passeth all understanding.

Buddha died 543 years before Christ was born and his teachings gradually lost their purity and simplicity. He became a god surrounded by legends and idol worship.

CHAPTER XIV

KUNDALINI YOGA
By Sri Swami Sivananda

Kundalini Yoga is that Yoga which treats of Kundalini Shakti, the six centres of spiritual energy (Shat Chakras), the arousing of the sleeping Kundalini Shakti (The mysterious Power of the Body).

All agree that the one aim which man has in all of his acts is to secure happiness for himself. The highest as well as the ultimate end of man must, therefore, be to attain eternal, infinite, unbroken, supreme happiness. This happiness can be had in one's own Self or Atman only. Therefore, search within to attain this eternal Bliss!

The thinking faculty is present only in human beings. Man only can reason, reflect and exercise judgment. It is man only who can compare and contrast, who can think of pros and cons and who can draw inferences and conclusions. This is the reason why he alone is able to attain God-consciousness. That man who simply eats and drinks and who does not exercise his mental faculty in Self-realization is only a brute.

Oh worldly-minded persons! Wake up from the sleep of Ajnana (ignorance). Open your eyes. Stand up to acquire knowledge of Atma (self). Do spiritual Sadhan (prayer-practice) ; awaken the Kundalini (mysterious powers).

During concentration you will have to collect carefully the dissipated rays of the mind. Vrittis (conflicting thoughts) will be ever-rising from the ocean of Chitta (consciousness). You will have to put down the waves as they arise. When all the waves subside, the mind becomes calm and serene. Then the

Yogi enjoys peace and bliss. Therefore real happiness is within. You will have to get it through control of mind and not through money, women, children, name, fame, rank or power.

Purity of mind leads to perfection in Yoga. Regulate your conduct when you deal with others. Have no feeling of jealousy towards others. Be compassionate. Do not hate sinners. Be kind to àll. Be trustworthy. Success in Yoga will be rapid if you put your maximum energy in your Yogic practice. You must have a keen longing for liberation and intense Vairagya (renunciation) also. You must be sincere and earnest. Intent and constant meditation is necessary for entering into Samadhi (superconscious state).

Nirvikalpa is the state of super-consciousness. This is the Goal of life. The aspirant gets knowledge of Self, supreme peace and infinite, indescribable bliss. This is also called Yogarooda state.

The Yogic student drinks the Nectar of Immortality. He has reached the Goal. Mother Kundalini has done her task now. Glory to Mother Kundalini! May her blessings be upon you all!

Om Santi!! Santi!!!

ESSENCE OF KUNDALINI YOGA

The word YOGA comes from the root Yuj which means to join, and in its spiritual sense, it is that process by which the human spirit is brought into near and conscious communion with, or is merged, in the Divine spirit.

The Yogi does not neglect his body. He realises in the pulsating beat of his heart the rhythm which throbs through and is the song of the Universal Life. To neglect or to deny the needs of the body; to think of it as something not divine; is to neglect and deny the greater life of which it is a part; and to falsify the great doctrine of the unity of all and of the ultimate identity of Matter and Spirit. Governed by such concept, even the lowliest physical needs take on a cosmic significance. Man when seeking to be the master of himself, seeks on all the planes; physical, mental and spiritual; nor can they be severed, for they are all related; being but differing aspects of the one all-pervading Consciousness. Who it may be asked is the more divine; he who neglects and spurns the body or mind that he may attain some fancied spiritual superiority, or he who rightly cherishes both as forms of the one Spirit which they clothe?

By the processes of Yoga, it is sought to attain a perfect physical body which will also be a wholly fitting instrument through which the mind may function. The Yogin thus seeks a body which shall be as strong as steel, healthy, free from suffering and therefore, long-lived. Master of the body he is; master of both life and death. His lustrous form enjoys the vitality of youth. He lives as long as he has the will to live and enjoys in the world of forms. His death is the death at will when he grandly departs.

FOUNDATION-VAIRAGYA

Man, ignorant of his true Divine nature, vainly tries to secure happiness in the perishable objects of this illusory sense-universe. Every man in this world is restless, discontented and dissatisfied. He feels actually that he is in want of something, the nature of which he does not really understand. He seeks the rest and peace that he feels he is in need of, in the accomplishment of ambitious projects. But he finds that worldly greatness when secured is a delusion and a snare. He doubtless does not find any happiness in it. He gets degrees, diplomas, titles, honors, powers, name and fame. He marries, he begets children; in short, he gets all that he imagines would give him happiness. But yet he finds no rest and peace.

Are you not ashamed to repeat the same process of eating, sleeping and talking again and again? Are you not really fed up with the dream objects created by the jugglery of Maya (illusion)? Have you a single sincere friend in this universe? Is there any difference between an animal and the so-called dignified human being with boasted intellect, if he does not do any spiritual Sadhana (prayer) daily, for Self-realization? How long do you want to remain a slave of passion, Indriyas, sex and body? Fie on those miserable wretches who revel in lust and who have forgotten their real Godlike nature and their hidden powers!

The so-called educated persons are refined sensualists only. Sensual pleasure is no pleasure at all. Illusions are deceiving you at every moment. Pleasure mixed with pain, sorrow, fear, sin, disease, is no pleasure at all. The happiness that depends upon perishable objects is no happiness. If your wife dies, you weep. If you lose money or property, you are drowned in sorrow. How long do you want to remain in that abject, degraded state? Those who waste their precious life in eating, sleeping and chatting without doing any Sadhana (praying) are brutes only.

You want supreme peace and happiness. This you will find in your realization of the Self only. Then alone will all your miseries and tribulations melt away. You have taken this body only to achieve this end. 'Din nike bitejate hain—The days are passing away quickly." The day has come and gone. Will you waste the night also?

"You are bound in this world by desires, actions and manifold anxieties. Therefore you do not know that your body is slowly decaying and wasting. Therefore wake up, wake up."

Now wake up. Open your eyes. Apply diligently to spiritual Sadhana (prayer). Never waste even a minute. Many Yogis and Jnanis, Dattatreya, Patanjali, Christ, Buddha, Gorakhnath, Matsyendranath, Ram Das and others have already trodden the spiritual path and realized through Sadhana. Follow their teachings and instructions implicitly.

Courage, Power, Strength, Wisdom, Joy and Happiness are your Divine heritage, your birth-right. Get them all through proper Sadhana. It will be simply preposterous to think that your Guru (teacher) will do the Sadhana for you. You are your own redeemer. Gurus and Acharyas will show you the spiritual path, remove doubts and troubles and give some inspiration. You will have to tread the Spiritual Path. Remember this point well. You will have to take each step yourself in the Spiritual Path. Therefore do real Sadhana (prayer).

Free yourself from death and birth and enjoy the Highest
Bliss.

WHAT IS YOGA?

The word "Yoga" comes from a Sanskrit root "Yuj" which
means to join. In its spiritual sense it is that process by which
the identity of the Jivatma (soul) and Paramatma (God-
spirit) is realized by the Yogis. The human soul is brought
into conscious communion with God. Yoga means restraining
the mortal desires. "Yoga is that inhibition of the functions of
the mind which leads to mortifying of the spirit in its real
nature. The inhibition of these fleshly desires of the mind
is by Abhyasa (practice) and Vairgya (renunciation and firmness)." (Yoga Sutras.)

Yoga is the Science that teaches the method of joining the
human spirit with God. Yoga is the Divine Science which dis-
entangles the Jiva (mind) from the world of sense objects
and links him with the Ananta Anand (Infinite bliss), Parama
Santi (Supreme Peace), joy of an Akhanda character and
Power that are inherent attributes of the Absolute.

Energy is wasted in too much talking, unnecessary worry
and vain fear. Gossiping and tall-talk should be given up
entirely. A real Sadhak (spiritual aspirant) is a man of few
words, to the point and that too on spiritual matters only.
Sadhaks should always remain alone. Mowna (silence) is a
great desideratum. Parties and talking with gossips are highly
dangerous for a Sadhak. The company of a gossip is more
injurious than immoral acts. Mind has the power to imitate.

YOGIC DIET

A Sadhak should observe perfect discipline. He must be
civil, polite, courteous, gentle, noble and gracious in his behavior. He must have perseverance, adamant will, patience and
leech-like tenacity in Sadhana (spiritual practice). He must
be perfectly self-controlled, pure and devoted to his goals.

A glutton or one who is a slave of his senses and bad habits
is unfit for the spiritual path.

"Without observing moderation of diet, if one takes to the Yogic practices, he cannot obtain any benefit but gets various diseases." (Ghe. Sam. V-16.) Food plays a prominent role in Yoga Sadhana. An aspirant should be very careful in the selection of articles of food. Purity of food leads to purity of mind. The discipline of food is very, very necessary for Yogic Sadhana. By the purity of food follows the purification of the inner nature; by the purification of the nature, memory becomes firm and on strengthening the memory, follows the loosening of worldly ties.

I will give you a list of foods for a Yoga.

Milk, red rice, barley, wheat, Havis Annam, Cheru, cream, cheese, butter, green dhal (Moongdal), Badam (almonds), vegetables, pomegranates, sweet oranges, grapes, apples, bananas, mangoes, dates, honey, dried ginger, etc., are the Sattwic articles of diet prescribed for the Yoga.

A fruit diet exercises a benign influence on the constitution. This is a natural form of diet. Fruits are very great energy-producers. Fruits help concentration and easy mental focussing. Barley, wheat, and ghee promote longevity and increase power and strength. Fruit juices are very good beverages. Almonds soaked in water can be taken.

FORBIDDEN ARTICLES

Sour, hot, pungent and bitter preparations, salt, mustard, chillies, meat, eggs, fish, cakes, sweets, alcoholic liquors, and other articles that disagree with your system should be avoided entirely.

Live a natural life. Take simple food that is agreeable. You should have your own Menu to suit your constitution. You are yourself the best judge to select a Yoga diet.

There is a general misapprehension that a large quantity of food is necessary for health and strength. Almost all diseases are due to over-eating and unwholesome food. Eating all things at all times is highly dangerous. Such a man can become a Rogi (sick man) easily; but he can never become a Yogi. Hear the emphatic declaration of Lord Krishna:—"Success in Yoga is not for him who eats too much." (Gita Chap. VI-16.)

Yoga Exercises

In the following pages I will tell you the different exercises that are intended to awaken the Kundalini (mysterious powers of the body). If you are wise enough, after a perusal of the different exercises, you can easily pick up the right method of sadhana (practice) that suits you best and attain success.

Before awakening the Kundalini, you must have Deha Shuddhi (purity of body), and Mano Suddhi (purity of mind). For the purification of the body, the following exercises are prescribed.

What Is Prana?

Prana is the sum total of all energy that is manifested in the universe. It is the vital force, Sukshma. Breath is the external manifestation of Prana. By exercising control over this gross breath, you can control the subtle Prana inside. Control of Prana means control of mind. Mind cannot operate without the help of Prana. It is the Sukshma Prana that is intimately connected with the mind. Prana is the sum total of all latent forces which are hidden in men and which lie everywhere around us. Heat, light, electricity, magnetism are all the manifestations of Prana. Prana is related to mind; through mind to the will; through will to the individual soul; and through this to the Supreme Being.

The seat of Prana is the heart. Prana is one; but it has many functions to do. Hence it assumes five names according to the different functions it forms, viz., Prana, Apana, Samana, Udana and Vyana. According to the different functions they perform, they occupy certain places in the body.

Breath directed by thought under the control of the will is a vitalising, regenerating force which can be utilized consciously for self-development, for healing many incurable diseases and for many other useful purposes. Hatha Yogins consider that

Prana Tattwa is superior to Manas Tattwa (mind), as Prana (vital energy) is present even when mind is absent during deep sleep. Hence Prana plays a more vital part than mind.

If you know how to control the little waves of Prana working through mind, then the secret of controlling matter will be known to you. The Yogin who becomes an expert in the knowledge of this secret, will have no fear from any power, because he has mastery over all manifestations of power in the Universe. What is commonly known as Power of Personality is nothing more than the natural capacity of a person to wield his Prana. Some people are more powerful in life, more influential and fascinating than others. It is all through this Prana, which the Yogin uses consciously by the command of his will.

BHASTRIKA

Rapid succession of forcible expulsions is a characteristic feature of this exercise. "Bhastrika" means "bellows" in Sanskrit. Just as a blacksmith blows his bellows rapidly, so also you should inhale and exhale rapidly. Sit in your favorite Asana (position). Close the mouth. Inhale and exhale quickly 20 times like the bellows. Constantly dilate and contract the chest as you inhale and exhale. When you practice the Pranayama a hissing sound is produced. You should start with forcible expulsions of breath following one another in rapid succession. After 20 such expulsions, make a deep inhalation and retain the breath as long as you can comfortably and then slowly exhale. This is one round of Bhastrika.

Begin with 10 expulsions for a round and increase it gradually to 20 or 25 for a round. The period of retention of breath also should be gradually and cautiously increased. Rest a while after one round is over and again begin the next round. Do 3 rounds in the beginning and after due practice, do 20 rounds in the morning and 20 in the evening.

Bhastrika removes inflammation of the throat, increases the gastric fire, destroys phlegm and all diseases of the nose and

197

lungs, eradicates Asthma, consumption and other diseases which arise from the excess of mucus. It gives warmth to the body. It is the most effective of all Pranayama exercises.

SIRSHASANA

(Headstand)

Spread a four-folded blanket. Sit on the two knees. Make a finger-lock by inter-weaving the fingers. Place it on the ground up to the elbow. Now keep the top of your head on this finger-lock or between the two hands. Slowly raise the legs till they become vertical. Stand on your head for five seconds in the beginning and gradually increase the period by 15 seconds each week to 20 minutes or half an hour. Then very slowly, come down. Strong people will be able to keep the Asana for half an hour within 2 or 3 months. There is no harm. If you have time, do twice daily both morning and evening. Perform this Asana very, very slowly, to avoid jerks. While standing on the head, breathe slowly through the nose and never through the mouth.

Sirshasana is really a blessing and a nectar. Words will fail to adequately describe its beneficial results and effects. In this Asana alone, the brain can draw plenty of Prana (vital energy) and blood. Memory increases admirably. Lawyers, occultists and thinkers will highly appreciate this Asana.

SARVANGASANA

(Shoulder Stand)

This is a mysterious Asana which gives wonderful benefits. Spread a thick blanket on the floor and practice this Asana over the blanket. Lie on the back. Slowly raise the legs. Lift the trunk, hips, and legs quite vertically. Support the back with the two hands, one on either side. Rest the elbows on the ground. Press the chin against the chest. Do not allow the body to shake or move to and fro. Keep the legs straight. In this Asana the whole weight of the body is thrown on the shoulders. You really stand on the shoulders with the help and

198

support of the elbows. Retain the breath as long as you can with comfort, and slowly exhale through the nose.

You can do this Asana twice daily morning and evening. Stand on the Asana for two minutes and gradually increase the period to half an hour.

BENEFITS

This is a panacea, a cure-all, a sovereign specific for all diseases. It brightens the psychic faculties and awakens Kundalini Shakti (The Mysterious Powers in the Body), removes all sorts of diseases of intestine and stomach, and augments the mental power.

It supplies a large quantity of blood to the roots of spinal nerves. It is this Asana which centralizes the blood in the spinal column and nourishes it beautifully. But for this Asana there is no scope for these nerve-roots to draw sufficient blood supply. It keeps the spine quite elastic. Elasticity of the spine means everlasting youth. It stimulates you in your work. It prevents the spine from early ossification (hardening). So you will preserve and retain your youth for a long time. Ossification is degeneration of bones. Old age manifests quickly on account of early ossification. The bones become hard and brittle in the degenerative process. This exercise acts as a powerful blood tonic and purifier. It tones the nerves. He who practices Sarvang is very nimble, agile, full of energy. The muscles of the back are alternatively contracted, relaxed and then pulled and stretched. Hence they draw a good supply of blood by these various movements and are well nourished. Various sorts of myalgia (muscular rheumatism), lumbago, sprain, neuralgia, etc., are cured by this Asana.

The vertebral column becomes elastic as rubber. The vertebral column is a very important structure. It supports the whole body. It contains the spinal cord, spinal nerve and sympathetic system. Therefore you must keep it healthy, strong and elastic. The muscles of the abdomen, and the muscles of the thigh are also toned and nourished well. Obesity or corpulence and habitual chronic constipation, gulma, congestion and enlargement of the liver and spleen are cured by this Asana.

PASCHIMOTTANASANA

Sit on the ground and stretch the legs stiff like a stick. Catch the toes with the thumb and index and middle fingers. While catching, you will have to bend the trunk forwards. Fatty persons will find it rather difficult to bend. Exhale. Slowly bend without jerks till your forehead touches your knees. You can keep the face even between the knees. When you bend down, draw the belly back. This facilitates the bending forwards. Bend slowly by gradual degrees. Take your own time. There is no hurry. When you bend down, bend the head between the hands. Retain it on a level with them. Young persons with elastic spine can touch the knees with the forehead even in their very first attempt. In the case of grown-up persons with rigid spinal column, it will take a fortnight or a month for complete success in the posture. Retain the breath till you take the forehead back, to its original position, till you sit straight again. Then breathe.

Retain the pose for 5 seconds. Then gradually increase the period to 10 minutes.

BENEFITS

This is an excellent asana. It reduces fat in the abdomen and makes the loins lean. This Asana is a specific for corpulence or obesity. It brings about reduction of spleen and liver in cases of enlargement of spleen. What Sarvangasana is for the stimulation of endocrin glands, so is Paschimottanasan for the stimulation of abdominal viscera, such as kidneys, liver, pancreas, etc. This Asana relieves constipation, removes sluggishness of liver, dyspepsia, belching and gastritis. Lumbago and all sorts of myalgia of the back muscles are cured. This Asana relieves piles and diabetes also. The muscles of the abdomen, the solar plexus, the epigastric plexus, bladder prostate, lumbar nerves, sympathetic cord are all toned up and kept in a healthy, sound condition.

MAYURASANA
(*Peacock Pose*)

This is more difficult than Sarvangasana. This demands good physical strength.

Kneel on the ground. Sit on the toes. Raise the heels up. Join the two forearms together. Place the palms of the two hands on the ground. The two little fingers must be in close touch. They project towards the feet. Now you have got steady and firm fore-arms for supporting the whole body in the ensuing elevation of the trunk and legs. Now bring down the abdomen slowly against the conjoined elbows. Support your body upon your elbows. This is the first stage. Stretch your legs and raise the feet stiff and straight on a level with the head. This is second stage.

Neophytes (beginners) find it difficult to keep up the balance as soon as they raise the feet from the ground. Place a cushion in front. Sometimes you will have a fall forwards and you may hurt your nose slightly. Try to slip on the sides when you cannot keep up the balance. If you find it difficult to stretch the two legs backwards at one stroke, slowly stretch one leg first and then the other. If you adopt the device of leaning the body forwards and head downwards the feet will by themselves leave the ground and you can stretch them quite easily. When the Asana is in full manifestation the body will be in one straight line and parallel to the ground. This posture is very beautiful to look at.

BENEFITS

This is a wonderful Asana for improving digestion. It cures dyspepsia and diseases of the stomach. The whole abdominal organs are properly toned and stimulated well by the increase of abdominal pressure. Sluggishness of liver disappears. It tones the bowels and removes constipation (ordinary, chronic and habitual). It awakens Kundalini.

INSTRUCTIONS ON ASANAS

1. Be regular in the practice. Those who practice by fits and starts will not derive any benefit.

2. Asanas should be done on empty stomach in the morning or at least three hours after food. Morning time is best for doing Asanas.

3. In the beginning you cannot perform some of the Asanas perfectly. Regular practice will give perfection. Patience and perseverance, earnestness and sincerity are needed.

4. If you are careful about your diet, Asanas and meditation, you will have fine, lustrous eyes, fair complexion and peace of mind in a short time. Hatha Yoga ensures beauty, strength and spiritual success to the Yogic students.

BHAKTI
(*Peace of Mind*)

Bhakti (peace of mind) can be acquired and cultivated. Practice of the Nava Vidha Bhakti (nine methods of devotion) will infuse Bhakti. Constant Sat Sang, Japa, Prayer, Meditation, Swadhyaya, Bhajan, Service to saints, Dana, Yatra, etc., will develop Bhakti. The following are the nine methods of developing Bhakti:

Sravan—hearing of the Voice of God. Smaran—remembering God always. Kirtan—singing His praise. Vandana—Namaskars to God. Archana—offerings to God. Pada Seavan—attendance. Sakhya—friendship. Dasya—services. Atma neivedhan—self-surrender to God.

Sri Ramanuja recommends the following measures of developing Bhakti: Viveka—discrimination. Vimoka—freedom from flesh desires and longing for God. Abhyas—continuous thinking of God. Kriya—doing good to others. Kalyana—wishing well to all. Satyam—truthfulness. Arjavam—integrity. Daya—compassion. Ahimsa—non-violence. Dana—charity.

POWER OF A YOGI

(*Minus Siddhis*)

A Yogi forgets the body in order to concentrate the mind on the Lord. He conquers heat and cold by mastering breath-control and by controlling his nervous system.

He can bear extremes of climates without discomfort.

DHARANA

(*Concentration*)

Fix the mind on some object either within the body or outside. Keep it there steady for some time. This is Dharana. You will have to practice this daily. Yoga has its basis on Dharana.

CONCENTRATION

Those who practice concentration evolve quickly. They can do any work with greater efficiency in no time. What others can do in six hours can be done easily in half an hour by one who has a concentrated mind. Concentration purifies and calms the surging emotions, strengthens the current of thought and clarifies the ideas. Concentration keeps a man in his material progress also. He will turn out very good work in his office or business-house. What was cloudy and hazy before, becomes clearer and definite; what was very difficult before becomes easy now; and what was complex, bewildering and confusing before, comes easily within the mental grasp. You can achieve anything by concentration. Nothing is impossible for one who regularly practices concentration. Clairvoyance, clairaudience, mesmerism, hypnotism, thought-reading, music, mathematics and other sciences depend upon concentration.

Retire into a quiet room. Close your eyes. Begin to concentrate on your goal. The mind may begin to entertain some other extraneous ideas. It may begin to wander. It may think of a show you saw the other night. It may think of going shopping. You should try to have a definite line of thought. There should not be any break in the line of thinking. You

203

must not entertain any other thoughts which are not connected with the subject on hand. The mind will try its level best to run in its old grooves. You will have to struggle hard in the beginning. The attempt is somewhat like going up a steep hill. You will rejoice and feel immense happiness when you get success in concentration.

For a neophyte the practice of concentration is tiring in the beginning. He has to cut new grooves in the mind and brain. After some time, say two or three months, he gets great interest. He enjoys a new kind of happiness. Concentration is the only way to get rid of the miseries and tribulations. Your only duty is to achieve concentration and through concentration to attain the final beatitude, Self-realization.

NAPOLEON BONAPARTE

Napoleon Bonaparte was a man of great concentration. His success was all due to the power of concentration. He suffered from various diseases as epileptic fits, Brady cardia, etc. But for these maladies, he would have proved still more powerful. He could sleep at any time he liked. He would snore the very moment he retired to bed. He would get up at the very second of the appointed time. This is a kind of Siddhi. He did no Vikshep or shilly-shallying. He had the highly developed Ekagrata mind of a Yogi. He could draw, as it were, any single thought from the brain pigeon-hole, dwell on it as long as he liked and shove it back when finished. He would sleep very soundly at night amidst busy war; would never worry a bit at night. This was all due to his power of concentration. Concentration can do anything. Without concentration of mind nothing can be achieved.

SECLUSION

If circumstances prevent you from observing Mowna (seclusion), strictly avoid long talk, conversations and all sorts of vain discussions and withdraw yourself from society as much as possible. Too much talk is simply wastage of energy. If this energy is conserved by Mowna (seclusion), it will be transmuted into Ojas Shakti (Spiritual Energy and Powers) which will help you in your Sadhana (meditations).

Sadhaka (The Spiritual Aspirant) should always remain alone. This is an important factor in spiritual progress. Mixing with people is dangerous. Solitude for Sadhana (spiritual exercises) is a great *desideratum*. All energies must be carefully preserved. After a short stay in solitude, aspirants should not enter the world. What they have gained in five years in seclusion through hard Tapas (exercises), will be lost in a month by mixing with worldly people. Several persons have complained to me that they have lost the power of concentration in this manner.

After attaining perfection in Yoga, one can enter the world if he is not affected by the unfavorable, hostile thought currents of the world. There is no harm if you mix with congenial company which is also devoted to Yoga. You can discuss various philosophical points. You can be in the company of higher spiritual personages who have entered into the Samadhi (spiritual state).

Everything must be done gradually. It is very difficult for a man who is in the world to be in entire seclusion.

Most of the difficulties arise in your daily life if you do not have a proper control over your mind. For instance, if a man does evil to you, instantly you want to revenge, to extract tooth for tooth, tit for tat policy; to return anger for anger. Every reaction of evil shows that the mind is not under control. By anger one loses his energy. A balanced state of mind is not possible. From anger all other impurities emanate. Anger transmuted into Love, becomes an energy so powerful as to move the whole world.

If you have the evil habit of drinking whisky, coffee, etc., and if you want to stop it, go to the meditation room and promise before the Deity that you will stop the bad habit from that moment. Proclaim this determination to your friends. If your mind goes to the same habit, you will naturally be ashamed to continue the habit. Several times you will fail. Still struggle hard. Study religious books. You can destroy all impure habits. If you find it very difficult to give up, the last remedy you will have to take is in running away from the present society and you must flee to a place where you cannot get all these. Out of compulsion you can leave the bad habit.

Develop the power of endurance (Titiksha). Learn to bear happiness and misery evenly and to pass through all phases of life and all experiences.

Humility is the highest of all virtues. You can destroy your egotism by developing this virtue alone. You can influence people. You will become a magnet to attract the world. It must be genuine. Feigned humility is hypocrisy. The River is mighty because it humbles itself below the mountain streams.

Control anger by practice of Kshama (concentration), Dhairya, patience and Nirabhimanata (profound meditation). When anger is controlled and replaced by Love, it will be transmuted into an energy by which you can move the whole world. Anger is a modification of passion. If you can control lust, you have already controlled anger. Drink a little water when you become angry. It will cool the brain and calm the excited, irritable nerves. Count twenty, one by one. By the time you finish counting twenty, anger will subside. Watch the small irritable impulse or thought-wave carefully. Then it will become more easy for you to control anger. Take all precautions. Do not allow anger to burst out and assume a wild form. If you find it extremely difficult to control it, go out and walk for half an hour. Pray to God. Meditate. Meditation gives immense strength.

Very often depression and discouragement comes in meditation in beginners owing to the influence of Samskaras (sense impressions), influence of astral entities, bad company, cloudy days, overloaded stomach. It must be removed by cheerful thoughts, a brisk walk, singing His Name, laughing, praying, and deep breathing.

If you want to enter into Samadhi quickly, cut all connections with friends, relatives, and others. Observe Akhanda Mowna (unbroken prayer). Plunge in meditation.

"Disease, mental inactivity, doubt, indifference, laziness,

tendency to go after sense-enjoyments, stupor, false perception, non-attainment of concentration and falling away from that when attained on account of restlessness, are the obstructing distraction." (Yoga Sutras I-30.)

If a practitioner is gloomy, depressed and weak, surely there is some error in his Sadhana (spiritual practices). If aspirants themselves are gloomy and peevish how can they impart joy, peace and strength to others? A cheerful and ever-smiling countenance is a sure sign of spirituality and Divine life.

Oh emotional, enthusiastic young aspirants! Do your Sadhana (spiritual practices) with patience, persevere until you attain the superconscious state. Master every stage in Yoga. Do not take up any higher courses before you completely master the lower steps.

By continence, devotion to Guru and steady practice, success comes in Yoga after a time. The aspirant should always be patient and persevering.

As soon as Kundalini (The mysterious power in the body) is awakened for the first time, a Yogi gets these six experiences which last for a short time—Ananda, spiritual bliss; Kampan, tremor of the body and limbs; Utthan, rising from the ground; Ghurni, divine intoxication; Murcha, fainting; Nidra, sleep.

Do not stop Sadhana (spiritual practices) when you get a few glimpses and experiences. Continue the practice till you attain perfection.

You can do nothing by a happy-go-lucky life. Draw a programme of daily routine. Then follow to the very letter at any cost. Then you are sure to succeed.

You first separate yourself from the body; then you identify yourself with the mind and then you function on the mental plane. Through concentration, you rise above body-consciousness; through meditation you rise above mind; and finally through Samadhi (The Superconscious State), you reach the goal.

Eliminate fear altogether by constantly raising an opposite current of courage in the mind. Constantly and intently think of courage. Fear is an unnatural, temporary modification on account of Avidya (ignorance).

Do not be carried away by name and fame (Kyati). Ignore all these trivial things. Be steady in your practice. Never stop Sadhana till the final beatitude (bliss) is reached.

Several aspirants in the name of Tapasya neglect the body. All possible care should be taken to keep the body in a healthy condition. A Sadhak should take more care than a worldly man, because it is with this instrument that he has to reach the Goal. At the same time he must be quite unattached to the body. That is the proper ideal.

CHAPTER XV

THE YOGI IDEAL MAN
OF CULTURE*

The cultured man is one who is developed on all planes. He is sound of body, self-respecting. He lives simply, having amply met the necessities of life and is an accepted member of society. He has curbed his egocentricity to the point where the interests of others are also important. He never, therefore, exhibits a lack of sympathy by imposing on others or boring them.

Emotionally he is what is called objective. His love for others is based on his understanding of their uniqueness. He does not try then to exploit or change others. He encourages them to fulfill their own life patterns. Such a love, based on freedom, is the true meaning of the term "respect." It is never possessive or clinging.

The good-will of a cultured man is genuine. He is warm-hearted, sympathetic and has a firm handclasp. He is never envious or vindictive. The envious have, at bottom, a real lack of true compassion for the objects of their envy. This gives their well-meaning attempts to "do good" or to "help others" a wooden quality. They therefore fail because they are not totally sincere.

The cultured man does not doubt his own powers and abilities. He is not plagued by that fear of failure and craving for recognition that characterizes the insecure. He is, therefore, free from irritability, anger and fear.

An uncultured or primitive person gets angry at every at-

* *The Teachings of the Buddhas,* by Dr. Garabed H. Paelian, published by Astara Foundation, Los Angeles, California.

tack or criticism because opponents appear powerful or wicked. This is because an unclarified mind represses its own faults and then projects them on all opponents. This creates a terrifying sight indeed. A person of discrimination would say with Khrishnamurti, "If he calls me a rascal it should give me insight to find out why he thinks so."

A cultured man is tolerant as he sees other viewpoints than his own. He does not consider it a loss of dignity to freely weigh the arguments of the opposition. He has poise, equilibrium, patience, fearlessness and a sense of order (relativity). Above all, these manifest as serenity.

Serenity is more than a social virtue. It is a cosmic attitude. It comes to him who sees the meaning of life and recognizes that there is a divine order. It is an attitude that sees beyond time and space and believes in the law of compensation. I believe that it means that the SUPERCONSCIOUS is active within a man. A man operating on the level of the MORTAL is operating on the level of the "survival of the fittest." He is motivated by envy. His progress means to attain what his immediate superior possesses. He resents both those who have more, and also those who block him from getting what he wants. Such a man cannot love and is always irritated. Others are either a threat to his pride or to his attainment of goals. A man who is in touch with his Superconscious knows theoretically, however, that Spirit means the "instant availability of everything." A sense of power and serenity in his consciousness tells him that he can have anything he wants. He feels secure.

The serene man, then, is one who has connected himself with the Positive Ground of the Universe. He can afford to be calm, fearless, as he realizes that there is no danger to one who knows God's law. Such a man can have anything he wants within that law (that is that does not harm another—which is the whole, including the doer himself).

Such a serene, confident man feels at one with the beauties of nature. He realizes that all manifestations are equally sacred materializations of the One Power operating at different speeds or vibrations. The Chinese called this cultured person "The Princely Man." He is "a follower of the Tao."

The great Science of India is Yoga. It is the Eastern equivalent of joining a monastery. Like St. Augustine, the Hindu believes "Thou hast made us for Thyself and we are restless until we find ourselves in Thee." The Indians believe that anything less than a streamlined spearhead of effort to realize God is a pitiful waste of one's precious human birth. They believe that the number of souls longing to incarnate outnumber the opportunities to do so. It is therefore sin to waste any time at all in accomplishing one's mission.

The Yogi who achieves union with God achieves also His omnipotence and omniscience. He knows everything and can do God-like things like growing a tree before your eyes and picking the fruit. Miracles like the latter, however, are considered in very poor taste unless it is necessary to rescue or heal someone. Powers are never exploited.

CHAPTER XVI

YOGI TEMPLES

A trip to a Yogi Temple high up in the Himalayas, the "Rooftop of the World," is described by Baird T. Spalding in his book *"The Life and Teachings of the Masters of the Far East,"* published by DeVorss and Company, Los Angeles, California.

"The temple is located on a high mountain peak, is built of rough stone, and is said to be over twelve thousand years old. It is in a perfect state of preservation and repair. It is one of the first temples erected by the Siddha teachers and was erected by them as a place where they could go and have perfect silence. The site could not have been better chosen. It is on the highest peak in that part of the mountains; the elevation above sea level is 10,900 feet and it is over 5000 feet above the valley floor. The last seven miles it seemed to me the trail was straight up. At times it led over poles that were supported by ropes fastened to boulders above, then thrown over the cliff's side; and these supported the poles that served as a trail. As we walked over these poles, I realized that we were at least six hundred feet in mid-air. At other times we were obliged to climb pole ladders supported by ropes from above. The last ascent was perpendicular for about three hundred feet and was accomplished wholly by pole ladders. When we arrived I felt as if I were on top of the world.

"We were up before the sun the next morning and when I stepped out on the roof of that temple I forgot all about the ascent of the night before. The temple was so situated at the edge of a bluff, that, when you looked out, you could see nothing for thousands of feet below, and it seemed as if the whole temple were suspended in mid-air. I had considerable difficulty in persuading myself to believe otherwise. In the distance we could see three mountains, upon which, I was told, temples similar to this were located, but they were so distant I could not make out the temples with my field glasses.

"After eating a hearty supper served by the attendants, we retired for the night, but not to sleep, for our experiences were beginning to make a deep impression upon us. Here we were nearly nine thousand feet in the air, with no human being near us, except the attendants, with not a sound except that of our own voices. There did not seem to be a breath of air stirring. One of my associates said, 'Do you wonder that they chose the locations of these temples as places of meditation? The stillness is so intense one can fairly feel it. It certainly is a place in which to meditate.'

"My two associates were soon asleep, but I could not sleep; so I arose, dressed, and went out on the roof of the temple, and sat down with my feet hanging over the wall. There was just enough moonlight filtering through the fog to eliminate the inky blackness that would have prevailed had not the moon been shining. There was just enough light to reveal the great, billowy fog banks rolling by, enough to remind me that I was not suspended in space, that somewhere way down, the earth was as ever, and that the place I was sitting upon was somehow connected with it."

GLOSSARY OF ORIENTAL
TERMS AND NAMES

AHURA MAZDA. God of the Zoroastrian religion of Persia.

AJNANA. Ignorance.

AKASA. A term with different meanings in the various branches of Indian philosophy. It may be used to describe the immaterial or astral form of the body; the basic material of the universe; or, sometimes, the sky.

ANALECTS OF CONFUCIUS. An ancient Chinese book containing many of the sayings of this great sage.

ANNA. An Indian coin of little value.

ARYANS. An ancient people who settled in India several thousand years ago, bringing with them a belief in a Heavenly Father.

ASANA. A posture or position taken by many yogis when they meditate. (Asana, in Sanskrit, means seat.) There are eighty-four basic postures used by the yogis, and each has many variations. They are considered difficult by most Westerners.

ASHRAM. A spiritual retreat or dwelling place of a holy man in India. Often the seer shares his ashram with his disciples.

ATMAN. The spirit of God within man; the higher self.

BHAGAVAD GITA. Literally, "The Song Divine"—one of the Sacred Books of the East, which, under the guise of relating the deeds of ancient men and the gods, sets forth teachings of profound metaphysical importance. Several fine translations are available in English.

BHAKTI-YOGA. The yoga of devotion.

BHIKKU. A disciple of Gautama Buddha who has given up all worldly possessions. Much of our literary heritage from Buddha consists of his counsel to the bhikkus.

BRAHMA. The Lord of the Universe; supreme deity of the Hindus.

BRAHMIN. The Hindu caste of priests, highest of all the castes in India.

BUDDHA, GAUTAMA. Buddha (c. 563 B.C.-483 B.C.) was a religious leader of India who preached that we can improve our lot in future existences if we lead blameless lives.

CHUANG-TZE. A Chinese mystic and philosopher who lived about four centuries before Jesus. A believer in Taoism (which see) and an eminent disciple of Lao-Tze, he taught a philosophy more idealistic than that preached by Confucius.

CLOUD OF VIRTUE. A phrase used by the Hindus to describe kaivalya, which see.

CONFUCIUS. A great Chinese sage and philosopher (551-479? B.C.) who taught a system of moral philosophy and ethics which centers about the Golden Rule of benevolence and urges an unceasing search for knowledge and wisdom.

DALAI LAMA. Supreme religious leader of Tibet.

DHAMMAPADA. One of the Sacred Books of the East containing the moral and metaphysical teachings of Buddha.

DHARANA. An Indian technique of concentration.

DHARMA. A Sanskrit word meaning, basically, law, but also religion and obedience to its laws.

DHYANA. The Sanskrit word for meditation; it is used in the religions of both Buddhists and Hindus.

DRAVIDIANS. Dark-skinned people of ancient India who were conquered by the Aryans when they invaded that land.

EIGHTFOLD PATH. The rules of Gautama Buddha for leading a better life.

GANDHI, MAHATMA. Gandhi (1869-1948) was a

Hindu political and religious leader who, like Ramakrishna (which see), taught there is one God behind all religions. He made considerable contributions to the cause of India's liberation from its colonial status.

GURU. A teacher of the mystic lore of the Orient.

HATHA-YOGA. The practice of exercises to develop exceptional physical powers and, often, spiritual ones as well.

INDRA. A Hindu god.

ISLAM. The religion of Mohammed; also, all those who believe in it.

ISSA. Oriental name for Jesus. Many Hindus believe that Jesus, during the "hidden years" before His baptism, visited India and Tibet and taught there.

JNANA-YOGA. The yoga of the mind.

KAIVALYA. The word used by the yogis to describe the fact that they have mastered the scientific control of the psyche or soul. It is defined by them as true spiritual consciousness or a state of infinite freedom. The yogi who has achieved kaivalya is said to have all knowledge and power in his grasp.

KARMA. A pious action. In the religions of the Buddhists and Hindus, good acts are important in improving one's condition in future lives.

KARMA-YOGA. The yoga of effort or work. It is concerned with benevolent or worthy actions for the purpose of securing an improvement in one's lot in future lives.

KSHATRIYA. A Hindu caste of warriors.

KUMBHAKA. Holding one's breath—a common part of the yogic breathing exercises, or pranayamas.

KUNDALINI. A mystic force, said by the Masters of the Far East to repose at the base of the spine.

LAO-TZE. A Chinese philosopher who lived six centuries before the birth of Christ. He is said to have been the founder of one of the great faiths of China, Taoism, which see.

MANTRA. An Oriental prayer or hymn.

MARA. The principle of evil; death.

MASTERS OF THE FAR EAST. An expression commonly applied to the yogis of India, both ancient and modern, but in this work frequently used in a broader sense to describe also the famous teachers of metaphysical knowledge in other Oriental lands, including China and Tibet.

MAYA. Illusion.

MENCIUS. A Chinese philosopher who lived about four centuries before the birth of Christ. He preached the doctrines of Confucius, placing emphasis upon the thought that man is benevolent by nature. A statue of Mencius is usually a feature of Confucian temples.

MOWNA. Silence.

NIRVANA. Supreme or celestial happiness, the state sought by the disciples of Gautama Buddha and obtained usually only as the reward for a life well lived.

OM. A Sanskrit word used in many Oriental prayers. It is said to contain the mystic names of three Hindu deities, Vishnu, Siva, and Brahma, which see.

ONE-POINTEDNESS. The ability to exclude from your mind all thoughts but the one you wish to be possessed by.

PARIAH. A Hindu of no caste—considered beyond the pale and an outcast. The pariahs are often called "untouchables"; persons belonging to castes, or the traditional orders of Indian society, will have no traffic with them.

PATANJALI. An ancient teacher of yoga whose system is still followed in India today.

POTALA. Palace of the Dalai Lama in Lhasa, capital city of Tibet. It contains a thousand rooms.

PRANA. The Sanskrit word for breath. In Vedic and later Hindu teachings it means the breath of life or the life principle; it is the vital force in ourselves and all other things.

PRANAYAMA. A breathing exercise of the yogis.

PURAKA. Inhalation, or breathing in—one step in performing a pranayama, or yogic breathing exercise.

PURUSHA. The spirit.

RAJA. A king or chief in India.

RAMAKRISHNA. A Hindu priest and mystic of the nineteenth century who regarded all religions as possessing the same validity. Kindliness was an essential part of his doctrine, and his own life was to no small degree modeled after that of Christ.

RECHAKA. Expelling the breath—often the conclusion of a yogic breathing exercise.

RIGVEDA. An ancient Sacred Book of the East.

SADDHU. A Hindu holy man who, following the example of Buddha and other holy men of the Orient, has renounced all earthly possessions. He gains his livelihood by teaching and begging alms.

SADHANA. Prayer. Spiritual practice.

SAMADHI. A state of bliss, or superconscious state; a trance in which a yogi has unusual spiritual experiences and attains higher knowledge.

SAMYAMA. The ability of a yogi to become a channel of Universal Power which can be regulated at will.

SANKHYA. One of the ancient seers of India, or his book.

SANSKRIT. Ancient language of the Aryans. The oldest of the Sacred Books of India are written in this tongue, which is still studied by the yogis as well as many scholars of the West. Latin, Greek, Persian, Gaelic, Russian, and the Germanic languages, including English, are related to Sanskrit; all are conjectured to be descended from a mother tongue lost in the mists of prehistoric times.

SANTI. Peace.

SIDDHIS. Powers acquired by Master Yogins to control body and mind so as to achieve union with Brahma and transcend human consciousness.

SIVA. A god of the Hindus; the "Destroyer."

SRI. A title of honor given in India.

SRI AUROBINDO. A world-renowned Indian sage, poet, and writer of the twentieth century. His profound *The Life Divine* and others of his writings are available in English.

SUDRA. Hindu caste of serfs and servants.

SUTRA. An aphorism. In this work the term generally refers to the Yoga Sutras of Patanjali, a Hindu seer and teacher of ancient times.

SVETASVATARA UPANISHAD. One of the Sacred Books of the East.

SWAMI. An Indian sage and teacher.

TAOISM. A Chinese philosophy which places emphasis upon the value of meditation and patience. In this system of thought, the experiences of the senses are regarded as illusory; only in renunciation of the things of this world is happiness to be found.

TRIMURTI. The Hindu trinity, consisting of the gods Brahma, Vishnu, and Siva.

TSONG-KAPA. A Tibetan lama and teacher of five centuries ago. He is said by some to have been influenced by Christian teachings.

UDANA. An Indian name for a vital nerve current in the lungs.

UPANISHADS. Sacred Vedic books of ancient India.

VAIRAGA. Renunciation.

VAISYA. Hindu caste of merchants, propertied farmers, money lenders, artisans, and herdsmen.

VARNA. Indian word for color.

VEDA. A Hindu word meaning knowledge. It forms part of the titles of some of the Sacred Books of the East, such as the Rigveda.

VEDANTA. The name applied to a number of Indian philosophies whose concern is to discover the true reality behind the appearances of things.

VEDIC. Pertaining to the ancient holy books of India, the Vedas, and the metaphysical and religious teachings set forth in them.

VISHNU. A Hindu deity; the "Preserver."

VIVEKANANDA. A Hindu sage and teacher of yoga.

VRITTIS. Conflicting thoughts.

YOGA. An Indian word which means "yoke"—the yoking of the individual to the great forces of Nature and the Universe. There are many systems of yoga, or disciplines of physical and mental conditioning, for achieving this goal.

YOGASANA. A yogic posture or asana. (See asana.)

YOGA SUTRAS. A book by Patanjali, Master Yogin of India. One of the famous books of the Orient, it is studied by millions who through it are shown the way to greater power.

YOGI, YOGIN. A Hindu sage or seer who has devoted his life to the mastery of one or more of the many systems of yoga. The yogis are the possessors of powers often held to be supernormal.

ZOROASTRIANISM. A religion of ancient Persia founded by a sage named Zoroaster.

The Secret of the Ages
By Robert Collier

What was the SECRET OF THE AGES? One of the foundation stones of the ancient Hebrew religion was that the knowledge of the SECRET enabled anyone who possessed it to perform the most marvelous deeds. The SECRET was revealed to Moses, taught by him to Aaron and by him handed down to the High Priests of Israel. It was the secret enshrined in the Holy of Holies. It was the supreme object of all attainment, for with it one could do anything. The possession of this SECRET enabled Moses to overcome all the might of the Pharaohs and enabled the prophets to cure the sick and defeat great armies.

The Kabalists believed that Jesus knew this SECRET and it was by its power that he and his disciples worked their miracles. But in the wholesale persecution of the Christians, it is believed that the knowledge of the SECRET perished and this fact accounts for the practical cessation of miracles after the third century of the Christian religion. But they also believe that to him who rediscovers it will come POWER OVER ALL THINGS—over sickness, over wealth, over happiness.

We believe that in *THE SECRET OF THE AGES* by Robert Collier, you will find:

1. An understanding of the Infinite Power that is within you.
2. The SECRET of Power that releases it, the secret key that establishes the contact. That understanding, that method, that KEY, that SECRET, may be yours.

THE GREATEST DISCOVERY OF MODERN TIMES

The Golden Key that can unlock doors for you lies idle in your own mind until you decide to take it out and put it to practical use. Here is the great message which has been brought to us by modern psychology and ancient religion:

There is nothing on earth you want that you cannot have—IF only you will mentally accept the fact that you CAN have it! There is nothing you cannot do—once your mind has accepted the fact that you can do it.

William James, the world-famous Harvard psychologist, estimated that the average man uses only about 10% of his actual potential mental power. Think of it! Only 10%! He has almost unlimited power—yet ignores 90% of it. Unlimited wealth all about him—and he doesn't know how to take hold of it. With God-like powers slumbering within him, he is content to continue in his daily grind—eating, sleeping, working—plodding through a dull, routine existence. Yet all of Nature, all of life, calls upon him to awake and bestir himself!

Since Robert Collier first wrote THE SECRET OF THE AGES, more than 700,000 copies have been sold—

•   •   •

222